Praise for *Making Sense of Adoption*

"The biggest problem for most adoptive families is talking to their children about alternative forms of family building. This book is badly needed and will help a lot of families with the stress of this task. Highly recommended for adoptive families."

Sharon Kaplan, executive director, Parenting Resources
co-author *Cooperative Adoption*

"Provides many examples of ways to present difficult information in a sensitive manner – sensitive to the child's needs, to the birthparents' struggles and to the adoptive parents' perspective. Professionals will find this book helpful in expanding their knowledge base both about children's needs and ways to aid adoptive families in helping their children understand their own personal life history."

Vera I. Fahlberg, M.D., pediatrician and therapist

"In this time of increasingly sophisticated methods of resolving infertility, little attention has been paid as to how parents might explain to their children in simple, affirming language, donor insemination, surrogacy, and *in vitro* fertilization. Nor have there been realistic guidelines available to parents as to what information to share with family members and the community regarding such matters. This groundbreaking book addresses these issues in an appropriate and sensitive manner and is a valuable reference for families and physicians who are thinking about the child who might be conceived in these different ways or raising such a child."

Claudia L. Jewett, child and family therapist,
author of *Helping Children Cope With Separation and Loss*

Making Sense of Adoption

A Parent's Guide

Lois Ruskai Melina

A Solstice Press Book

Harper & Row, Publishers, New York
Grand Rapids, Philadelphia, St. Louis, San Francisco
London, Singapore, Sydney, Tokyo, Toronto

FIRST EDITION

A Solstice Press book produced at North Country Book Express, Inc., by Mary Schierman, Joyce Colvin, Karla Fromm, Melissa Rockwood, Kristin Mullally and Lisa Payne under the direction of Patricia Hart and Ivar Nelson.

Designed by Melissa Rockwood and Karla Fromm

Library of Congress Cataloging in Publication Data

Melina, Lois Ruskai
   Making sense of adoption : a parent's guide / Lois Ruskai Melina.

     p.   cm.
   Includes index.
   ISBN 0-06-055138-0
   ISBN 0-06-096319-0 (pbk.)
   1. Adoption – United States.   2. Children, Adopted – United States – Family relationships.   3. Child rearing – United States.   I. Title.
HV875.55.M438   1989
362.7'34'0973 – dc20   89-45106

89 90 91 92 93 FG 10 9 8 7 6 5 4 3 2 1
89 90 91 92 93 FG 10 9 8 7 6 5 4 3 2 1 (pbk.)

To Carl,
my partner in parenting

Acknowledgments

This book could not have been written without the understanding and cooperation of my family. They have been tolerant of my absences, whether that meant traveling around the country to talk to adoptive parents or disappearing into the basement to write.

I also want to express my appreciation to all the birth-parents, adoptees, adoptive parents, and professionals who have shared their questions, solutions, concerns, and personal stories with me, both at workshops and in personal interviews. Their experiences have enriched this book.

Hilary Hanafin, Glenda Hinton, Candace Turner, and Carol Frost Vercollone put me in touch with many individuals willing to talk about their experiences with donor insemination, surrogacy, and *in vitro* fertilization.

Claudia Jewett, Vera Fahlberg, Reuben Pannor, Sharon Kaplan, and Holly van Gulden Wicker have shared much wisdom and experience with the adoption community and with me personally over the years, and were willing to share more by reading the manuscript for this book and making suggestions for its improvement. I can't thank them enough.

Linda Rasmussen at the Moscow-Latah County Public Library did an extraordinary amount of work finding books for me so that I could review them for the Bibliography of Children's Books.

My capable assistants Shawn Poovey and Christine Lothen helped me with this book in more ways than I could enumerate.

Finally, special thanks to Nancy, Carolyn, and the others, who have helped me understand the importance of allowing children to express their feelings.

"Children are most like us in their feelings and least like us in their thinking."

–David Elkind
in *Children and Adolescents*

Contents

1. A Few Words for Parents

I was having dinner out with my children, who are both Asian–American. At a nearby table were three Asian–American women. My son, then three, pointed at the women and commented on their appearance. Before I could respond to him, my daughter, who was six, urgently whispered to him, "Be quiet. One of them could be your mother."

I knew then that my daughter was thinking about adoption and about her birthmother more frequently and with more depth than I was aware of.

This surprised me because she seemed to feel comfortable talking about adoption with me. She seemed willing to ask questions, and I thought I had let her know by my general responsiveness that we could talk about anything related to her adoption or her birthparents. And because I'm involved with adoption professionally, I thought I was, if anything, over-sensitive to any signs that she was dealing with an adoption issue.

For the first time, I realized that while we discussed adoption easily, she didn't share all her thoughts with me. And I knew that her thoughts at the age of six were only the beginning of years of questioning and increasing awareness about adoption and its importance in her life.

Shortly after that incident I began traveling throughout the country speaking to adoption groups about raising adopted children. Everywhere I went I found adoptive parents who want to help their children make sense of adoption in a way that leaves the children feeling self-assured and loved. Some were parents of infants and were anticipating the different concerns their children would have as they grew up. Others had already been asked specific questions by their preschoolers, school-age children, or adolescents.

This book, then, grew out of current child development theory and modern adoption philosophy, and out of the many conversations I have had with adoptive parents, adoptees, and birthparents.

It will help adoptive parents understand the kinds of concerns children have about themselves and their origins at each stage of growth so parents can provide the answers children need, even if the questions are not asked directly. Sample conversations and examples will help alert parents to subtle signs that their children could be grappling with adoption issues so accurate and age-appropriate information can be provided in a loving and empathetic way.

The information we provide our children affects them emotionally. Adoptive parents should be prepared not only for the questions their children will have, but for the reactions their children may have to the answers to those questions. Help in preparing for this role is offered later in this chapter.

Who needs this book

This book is for those parents who made a decision to become the legal parents of a child genetically unrelated to them, regardless of whether legal action was necessary for them to do so. It is for families who meet the dictionary's definition of adoption—to take and treat as one's own—regardless of whether they meet a court's definition.

This definition includes children adopted by stepparents; those conceived through donor insemination, *in vitro* fertilization with a donor egg or embryo, and surrogacy; as well as those who meet the traditional definition of adoption. (We sometimes distinguish between those adoptions in which birthparents and adoptive parents are not given the opportunity to share information or have ongoing contact and those in which information is shared and ongoing contact provided for by calling the former "traditional adoptions" and the latter "open adoptions." In this book, however, the term "traditional adoption" refers to the common practice of adoption – whether open or not – in which a child is legally adopted by one or two biologically unrelated parents, to distinguish it from adoption through donor insemination, surrogacy, and *in vitro* fertilization.)

Regardless of how children are adopted, they share important issues. For the preschooler, the question, "Where did I come from?" is more complex, either because of the method of conception or the child's journey to a new family after birth. School-age children wonder why they were adopted when most people aren't, and how their value as a person is affected by the different way they joined their families. Adolescents struggle to know who they are in a very basic sense – a question that is more difficult when they are missing information about their biologic parents.

Most importantly, adopted children are likely to grieve for the loss of their birthparents. This is not necessarily the same kind of grief they would feel if they suddenly lost the parents they had lived with for many years. It's a grief that comes from knowing they have lost people who played a significant role in their lives.

Even children who have regular contact with their birthparents, such as those in an open adoption, have lost their birthparents as parents, and may still have questions about why their birthparents didn't keep them and what it means to be adopted.

While adopted children share many issues, they also have issues unique to the particular way they joined their families. For example, children adopted through donor insemination, surrogacy, and *in vitro* fertilization with a donor egg or donor embryo were deliberately created by a parent intending to terminate his or her parental rights. In some cases, large sums of money were connected to the adoption. Other children had birthparents whose parental rights were taken away from them.

Parents who have adopted through donor insemination, surrogacy, and *in vitro* fertilization are just beginning to look toward the traditional adoption community for guidance in helping their children deal with these many issues because the importance of openness has been accepted in traditional adoptions for much longer. This book, however, goes beyond the standard advice given to adoptive families for many years – to tell their children early that they are adopted – and describes how children's awareness of adoption changes with their growth and suggests how parents can meet the challenges this poses in their families.

The rights of adopted children

Some time ago I was asked to write an essay on the rights of adopted children for the alternative parenting journal *Nurturing Today* (187 Caselli Ave., San Francisco, Calif. 94114). It was a topic I hadn't given much thought to. As I researched the article and examined my own thoughts on the subject, I came to the conclusion that children aren't accorded many rights at all. And those that they are given are subject to interpretation if they conflict with the rights of others. For example, children's right to a good education may conflict with the right of citizens not to be taxed excessively. And even when there is general agreement on children's rights, society is reluctant to impose its values on families who do not agree. For example, behavior that many people would consider child abuse is considered acceptable discipline by others.

So while I believe that adopted children have certain rights, these are not guaranteed by law. They can only be accorded to children if we are committed to the principles behind them:

1. *Children have the right to know who they are and how they joined their families, and to grow up knowing the truth.*

While some well-meaning people think children are "better off" believing their adoptive parents are their biologic parents, I think that's only true if we feel there is something wrong with being adopted. The truth may bring some sadness and pain, but there are far worse ramifications of dishonesty. Healthy relationships, including those in a family, can only be built on trust and honesty. Furthermore, if adoption is kept a secret, children are likely to realize there is something about them that nobody talks about and be unnecessarily concerned about what it might be. When such a secret is finally revealed, it can destroy relationships in the family. (The effect of secrecy on the child is discussed in Chapter 8.)

On the other hand, truthfulness is not an all or nothing affair. Young children do not need all the details about their origins or adoption. Some of the details will have to wait until children are mature enough to understand the facts and deal with the implications. The important point is that children should never knowingly be told or allowed to believe something that will later be contradicted by the truth–a point I refer to repeatedly in this book.

2. *Children have a right to freely ask questions and express their feelings about being adopted.*

Adoption is not a single event in the life of a family, but a different way of forming a family that affects that family forever. It is important to establish an attitude in the family that conveys to the child: "You can always talk about your birthparents and your adoption. You can always expect your questions to be answered honestly and appropriately. You can always express your feelings about your origins and your adoption."

3. *Children have a right to a positive attitude about their birthparents.*

How birthparents are portrayed affects children's feelings about themselves. If children think they came from "bad people," they are likely to think they are bad, too. This doesn't mean that we should idealize the birthparents or misrepresent them. It does mean we should educate ourselves so we can be more empathetic toward the birthparents. Once we do that, it is easier to portray birthparents as unique individuals rather than as stereotypes, and separate their actions, which may have been mistakes, from their innate value as human beings. Similarly, the decision to place a child for adoption should be portrayed in a positive way.

4. *Children have the right to be accepted as individuals with a unique genetic heritage.*

Our actions with our children, not just our words, must reflect that we are not only happy that they are who they are, with their unique mix of hereditary and environmental influences, but that we wouldn't have them any other way. Before we can do this, we have to let go of our fantasies about the child we expected to conceive and give birth to. When we let go of our expectations, we find that one of the most rewarding aspects of adoption is discovering who our children are.

5. *Children have a right to be recognized by society as full and equal members of their adoptive families.*

In the United States, families formed by adoption are still considered unusual, and therefore, not as good as traditional families. We are scrutinized carefully for signs that the parent–child relationship, formed in such an unusual way, is not as strong or as fulfilling as that in a traditional biologic family. Children have a right to grow up without having to justify (by exceptional behavior or achievements) belonging to their families and without expectations based on myths and stereotypes.

6. *Information about our children's origins is private information that belongs to them.*

While we should never hide the fact that a child is adopted, we should respect the child's right to privacy with regard to details about her birthparents and how she came to be adopted.

With rare exceptions, if any, the person who is adopted should have all the available information about her origins and adoption by the time she is an adult. I fully support the decision of adults to search for more information about their origins, including meeting their birthparents, even when it conflicts with the desires of the birthparents or the adoptive parents.

7. *Transracially adopted children have a right to a positive sense of racial or ethnic identity.*

Transracially adopted children should have an opportunity to learn about their race or ethnic group and be proud of being a member of it. They also have a right to feel competent in dealing with the discrimination and prejudice they will encounter as members of minority groups.

Parents' attitudes toward discussing adoption

Before our children understand what we say about adoption they will understand how we feel about it. Young children may have difficulty understanding the technology that led to their creation, or the social factors that influenced their birthparents to place them for adoption, but they will have no doubts about whether their parents are comfortable talking about these topics.

It isn't surprising that many parents are not entirely comfortable talking about adoption. Adoption involves talking with children about complicated, sensitive, private, and emotional subjects, such as reproduction, finances, and racial attitudes.

But if children perceive their parents are uncomfortable discussing adoption, they may conclude that there is something wrong with being adopted. They may also decide that if adoption makes their parents feel so uncomfortable, they shouldn't talk about it. That's just the opposite of the way we want our children to feel.

Some parents inadvertently convey a sense of uneasiness in discussing adoption because they are trying to present information in a way that ensures the child will never feel any sadness, pain, or rejection as a result of what they are told.

To expect that we can explain adoption without our children feeling any sadness or pain is to expect the impossible of ourselves and of our children. There are no "right words" to use to discuss adoption or "right time" to say them that will spare a child sadness, although some ways of discussing adoption are more positive than others. Adoption carries with it some sadness for everyone involved, and this must be acknowledged. Our children have been separated from significant people in their lives – the very people who gave them life. The fact that they might never have known these people is in itself cause for great regret. We as adoptive parents have felt sadness, too, because we are unable to have biologic children, or because we did not give birth to our children or spend their early weeks, months, or years with them.

Of course, adoption also involves great joy and satisfaction for those involved. Acknowledging the sadness and pain in adoption doesn't mean denying the joy. And acknowledging the joy doesn't mean we must deny the sadness.

As parents, we might hope that our children would feel

only joy in life, but that isn't realistic. We can't and shouldn't try to "protect" our children from honest emotions. What we can do is help our children learn how to cope with disappointment, confusion, sadness, and pain. We can help them make sense out of their confusion and comfort them in their sadness. What we must understand is that even though our children might at times feel uncomfortable, confused, or sad as a result of the way they joined their families, experiencing sadness or discomfort doesn't have to affect our children's overall self-esteem. And we don't have to feel guilty that they are feeling sadness or pain because we chose to adopt them.

What children want to know and can understand about adoption

Children who have been adopted have varying levels of interest in adoption and in their origins. They react in individual ways to information about their pasts. And they have varying degrees of curiosity and levels of determination in pursuing answers to their questions.

Furthermore, children's ability to understand various aspects of adoption changes with their development. Therefore, our goal is to provide information appropriate to children's ability to absorb it in a meaningful way, according to their interest and emotional maturity. This means that at times we will be providing our children with information that is new to them. At other times we will be providing them with information they have heard before, but in a way that reflects their mental or emotional growth.

The eight-year-old who says, "I wonder if I have any brothers and sisters I don't know about," probably wants different information from the fifteen-year-old *who asks the same question:* The younger child is likely to be interested in who her family is; the adolescent may be concerned that she is unknowingly dating a sibling or half-sibling.

It is not our children's responsibility to ask questions in ways that make this distinction clear to us. Most of us are not direct when we seek information. Asking a spouse, "How much do you think we should spend on Christmas presents for each other this year?" could mean anything from, "I'm concerned about finances and think we should be frugal," to "I've found something wonderful for you but I'm not sure I should spend that much money." Similarly, children are not always direct when they ask a question, especially when they're not exactly sure what they want to know. So when it comes to a complicated and emotional issue like adoption, we have to be prepared to anticipate our children's needs, clarify their questions, and provide them with the information they are really seeking.

How to use this book

This book is organized by developmental stages, beginning with infancy, to help parents recognize and anticipate the issues their child is likely to be dealing with at a particular time.

To use this book most effectively, parents should read it in its entirety and not assume that because they have an infant they don't need to read the section on adolescents yet, or because they have an adolescent they can skip the information about children in middle childhood.

Parents of young children will want to know about their child's current development stage and also how to anticipate their child's needs for information in the future.

Parents of an older child – including the child adopted at an older age – will want to know the kinds of issues their child is likely to have had in the past in case she did not have an opportunity to have those questions answered or express the feelings she was having at the time.

Of course, it is always important to remember that children are unique and develop at their own rate. Any book that describes how children are likely to be at different developmental stages must be read as a guide, with the understanding that your child may move into and out of these stages a little faster or a little slower than other children.

Because many children adopted at an older age have missed early developmental experiences due to neglect, abuse, or the lack of consistent parenting, their emotional and mental ages are often younger than their chronological ages. Parents should talk to them about adoption, and other topics, in ways appropriate for their mental and emotional ages.

Children who are developmentally delayed and who are adopted also deserve to know the truth about how they joined their families. While they may never be able to comprehend the full story of their adoption, they can and should be given information about their origins that is appropriate to their emotional and mental development.

You know your child and your family situation better than anyone else. One child will look at every person at a restaurant as a potential birth relative. She may quietly ponder the possibility for days or weeks without ever talking about it. Another child will deal with the same issue in a matter of seconds. Still another child might say to her parents or to her sibling: "Wouldn't it be funny if my birthmother were eating dinner at the same place that I was and we didn't even know it?"

This book, therefore, can only provide guidelines. If you question whether a suggestion in this book is appropriate for your child or your family, use your own judgment. Parents should be informed and should seek advice on all aspects of parenting, but should temper that information and advice with knowledge of their own family.

One final point needs to be made about how to use this book: Because most parents know the importance of allowing their children to express their thoughts and feelings about being adopted, they may be more sensitive to their children's need to talk about adoption than about other important subjects. Children are likely to feel rejected, sad, confused, angry, scared, or lonely in situations other than those relating to adoption. *If children only have an opportunity to talk about their feelings when they relate to adoption, they may think that all their feelings have something to do with adoption.* By recognizing the kinds of thoughts and feelings children have about adoption, parents can learn to respect the intellectual and emotional development of children in general. What parents learn about helping children express their concerns about adoption can serve as a model for helping children express their thoughts and feelings in other situations.

Activity: Getting ready

Some parents tell me they always planned to adopt. Others grew up in adoptive families themselves. Many of us once rejected adoption as a way of forming a family. Our attitudes toward adoption, as with other aspects of life, are influenced by our personal experiences, the family values we grew up with, the messages we have received from society, and informal and formal education.

Parents will be better able to meet their children's need to have adoption information presented to them in a realistic yet empathetic way if they first understand their own feelings about adoption.

You may want to explore your feelings about adoption privately, through informal discussion with a spouse, friend, or partner, or in a more structured way with an adoptive parents' group. However you choose to do it, keep in mind that you do not need to have resolved every issue or feel comfortable with every topic to talk with your child about adoption. That's an unrealistic expectation. Furthermore, remember that it's natural for some issues that seemed resolved at one time to crop up again at another time. For example, it isn't unusual for some infertility issues to re-emerge for parents when their children enter their reproductive years.

Understanding how we felt initially about different aspects of adoption and how those feelings may have changed can help us recognize any aspects of our adoption experience that may still be affecting our self-image and our expectations of our children. It can also help us prepare for how we will talk about these topics with our children. The following topics are important issues for adoptive families, although not all of them are appropriate to every family's situation and experience.

Infertility

People react to infertility in individual ways. For some people, the hardest part of infertility is being unable to experience or participate in a pregnancy. For others, the lack of control over a basic human function is most troubling. For others, the knowledge that they will never have a genetic descendant is hard to accept.

One parent may find that his experience with infertility taught him that he does not have control over all aspects of his life, while another may find himself wanting to have more control in those areas of his life in which he does have control. Another parent may find that her desire to experience pregnancy was satisfied by acting as a childbirth coach for her child's birthmother.

A woman who is infertile as a result of a sexually transmitted disease would want to think about how she will explain her reasons for adopting in an honest way that still protects her privacy.

Some parents have found that continued involvement with Resolve, Inc., an education and support group for infertile couples, helps them resolve ongoing infertility issues they may have, even after they have formed their families. (For more information on Resolve, Inc., see Appendix A: "Do We Need More Help?")

The decision to adopt

There's a big difference between the couple who feels comfortable adopting but chooses donor insemination because health insurance would pay the costs of a pregnancy but not the costs of a traditional adoption, and the couple who chooses donor insemination because the husband doesn't want people to know he is infertile. The first couple may be able to acknowledge the child's birthfather as a real person, but the husband in the second example may resent the birthfather's role in the conception of his child or even pretend the birthfather doesn't exist.

Some parents are initially attracted to intercountry adoption because, they reason, if the child is obviously adopted no one will hold them responsible for the child's behavior. Others want to adopt an infant because they believe environmental influences are so strong that they can mold the child to fit their expectations. In both cases, these parents may believe people will judge them by their children's behavior or accomplishments, which could result in unrealistic expectations of themselves and their children.

Reactions of family and friends

When we become parents, we are often surprised to see that we share more values with our parents than we thought we did. Looking back at the reactions our family and friends had to our decision to adopt can be clues to our own feelings.

For example, if we received a message from our family that a child who is adopted is likely to come from a family "not as good" as ours, then perhaps we unconsciously share that same concern.

When we are hurt by references to our child's "real mother," some of our pain results from knowing our society does in fact consider adoptive parents something less than real. But if we find ourselves getting unusually angry when someone asks about our child's "real mother," perhaps that reflects our own doubt about whether an adoptive family is really as good as a biologic family.

Reading about child-rearing practices in other cultures, for example, in which children are raised on a kibbutz or informal adoption is commonplace, has helped some parents realize that not all societies have the same attitude toward biologic families as ours. Learning more about bonding and attachment has reassured other parents that the quality of the parent–child relationship is not determined by the circumstances of the child's birth.

The birthparents' decision

Those of us who are infertile once placed a great deal of importance on becoming pregnant and giving birth to a child. Many of us were angry when we realized that despite all our efforts to conceive and carry a pregnancy to term, we were not being successful, while thousands of teenagers were being successful with little thought to what they were doing. Sometimes I wonder how we can talk with empathy and understanding about the teenager who placed her child for adoption if we once felt anger and resentment toward girls in similar situations. I wonder how we can discuss the birthmother's decision to place her child for adoption when we would have stood on our heads for nine months if that's what a doctor told us was necessary to deliver a baby. We're certainly glad that our child's birthmother placed her for adoption, and we probably believe it was the best decision for her and her child. But that isn't the same as being able to understand how she could decide to place her child for adoption.

Those parents who have had an opportunity to meet the birthmother and get to know her may be better able to explain her situation and decision in a positive manner. Many parents have not had that opportunity, however, and find that their understanding of the birthmother is enhanced by reading books like *To Love and Let Go* by Suzanne Arms (New York:

Alfred A. Knopf, 1983), and first-person accounts of birth-mothers, such as *Birthmark* by Lorraine Dusky (New York: M. Evans and Company, 1979), and by listening to birth-mothers speak at conferences, at pre-adoption sessions, or on videotapes, such as those available through Children's Home Society of Minnesota (2230 Como Ave., St. Paul, Minn. 55108). Parents of a child born in a foreign country often find it helpful to learn more about the attitudes toward women experiencing a crisis pregnancy in their child's country of origin.

Parents of children adopted through donor insemination or through *in vitro* fertilization with a donor egg or embryo can also examine what they think the birthparent's motives were. If we believe the sperm, egg, or embryo donors were acting out of empathy for other infertile couples or out of concern that a potential life not be destroyed, we are more likely to convey their decision as a positive plan.

Attitudes toward birthparents

What we believe and how we feel about our children's birthparents could very easily show up not only in the way we talk about them to our children, but in our expectations of our children. (See "Assuming the birthparents' identity" in Chapter 6.)

Some parents may have negative feelings about birth-parents based on stereotypes. We tend to resort to stereo-types when we lack information or personal experience with particular people. So obtaining more information from the adoption intermediary, reading about birthparents, or listening to them speak at conferences or on videotapes can help dispel some of these stereotypes.

Some parents have negative feelings about the birth-parents because the birthparents have had serious problems with drugs, alcohol, sexual exploitation, or abuse. But even in those situations, parents have been able to portray birth-parents in ways that neither glorify them nor condemn them.

(See "Explaining difficult situations" in Chapter 4 and "Developing a factual basis for identity" in Chapter 6.)

One way to think about how your child would want to hear about birthparents with serious personal problems is to imagine how you might talk with your child about a member of your family who is an alcoholic, a shoplifter, or a criminal. For example, you wouldn't condone Aunt Bertha's alcoholism, but you probably would want your child to know the positive aspects of Aunt Bertha, too, such as the time she took you to the seashore. You would probably want your children to forgive Aunt Bertha for her mistakes, but love her. After all, "she's family." That's how important the birthparents are to a child.

Heredity and environment

How much genetics influences intelligence, talents, personality, and temperament is still unclear. It appears that both heredity and environment are influential. Many adoptive parents, however, tend to minimize the effects of genetics, preferring to believe that the environment they provide their child will be more important than any innate abilities or characteristics. In many respects, this is a productive attitude to have. It helps us provide our children with opportunities and encouragement. But it can also send some messages to children that we don't intend to send, such as: "The child I would have given birth to would have been like this. For me to be happy with you, you have to be like this, too," or "I don't like what you got from your birthparents, I want you to be different." Unrealistic expectations like these doom our children to failure – something no parent wants to do. Many parents, therefore, find it helpful to remember that both genetics and environmental factors influence children.

Your child

When we expect to have a child who is genetically related to us, some of our expectations are based on the characteristics we expect to pass on to our children, such as red hair or a tall, slender frame. Indeed, one of the motivations for having children is that people who are in love with each other want a child who represents a joining of the two of them. When people find they are unable to reproduce themselves genetically, their second choice is frequently to have a child as close as possible to the child they would have produced genetically. This is one reason adoption through donor insemination, surrogacy, or *in vitro* fertilization appeals to many people. It's also why many prospective adoptive parents think first about adopting an infant who is racially like them. Recognizing what you or your spouse wanted to pass down to the next generation can help you understand the expectations you may have of yourselves and your children.

Parents and children are usually happier when children are not only accepted as the unique individuals they are, but when that individuality is cherished. Then, rather than expecting children to fulfill our fantasies, we can embrace the important task of parenthood – guiding children to develop themselves in the direction in which they are inclined and finding joy in their unique growth.

Discussing differences

People who are adopted feel different because they joined their families in a nontraditional way. Whether this difference is disturbing to them or is integrated into their self-image with ease depends to some extent on whether the important people in their lives believe differences are enriching or to be avoided. We help our children feel comfortable being adopted not only by discussing adoption in empathetic terms but by accepting religious, racial, physical, and economic differences in people.

2. "How Do We Begin?"
Infants and Toddlers, Family and Friends

From the very moment you become a family you will be talking about how your child joined your family. Many of these discussions will be with your child. Although infants and toddlers don't understand what it means to be adopted, most experts recommend introducing the subject right away. In these early years, these talks generally will be one-sided, brief, and simple. But they provide the foundation for more in-depth discussions later.

While your infant or toddler will not understand what it means to be adopted, others do, and from the beginning you will find yourself talking about your child's adoption with relatives, friends, other children in the family, and strangers. Being ready for these encounters will give you the confidence you need to discuss sensitive and personal matters with people both outside the family and within.

Parents who adopt children of a different racial or ethnic background tell me they frequently find themselves answering questions they feel unprepared for about adoption and their families because they are so obviously different from other families. I remember how shocked my husband was when he took our daughter for a walk shortly after her arrival and encountered a man who stared intently at the two of them before asking, with a wave of his hand toward our daughter, "Is your wife one of those?" (We've always been sorry he didn't reply, "A baby? No, my wife isn't a baby.")

Your child's early years are a good time to examine what it means to be a minority family and to begin introducing aspects of other cultures into your family life.

Starting early

I'm often asked by parents when they should tell a child he's adopted. Being adopted is part of the child's identity and part of the family's history. As such, adoption should be discussed matter-of-factly whenever appropriate.

Imagine how silly it would be to ask: "When should I tell my child he's a boy?" We start from the very first moment with our child to send him messages about his gender. We might say, "Where's my little boy?" or "What a handsome little boy!" The infant or toddler doesn't understand the difference between girls and boys, but that doesn't stop us from letting him know that he is a boy. Gradually, he learns that there are physical differences between boys and girls, and eventually (and sometimes to our dismay) that society has different expectations for boys and for girls. But even those who believe in nonsexist childrearing wouldn't dream of avoiding any mention of their child's gender, only to reveal to him on the eve of the first day of kindergarten that some children are boys and some are girls and that he is a boy.

The same is true of a child who is adopted. There are natural ways to talk about how a child joined a family that can and should be used even when the child is an infant and cannot understand what adoption means.

Besides providing your child with a general awareness of having been adopted, early discussions of adoption have two main purposes. The first is to create a feeling within the family that adoption is a topic for conversation. Infants and toddlers may not be able to understand what it means to be adopted, but they do understand whether mom and dad are comfortable talking about it.

The second purpose is to give parents a chance to practice talking about a topic that involves sensitive and sometimes painful issues. In the beginning it is common to have difficulty discussing some aspects of adoption. That's why it makes more sense to do so first with an infant, who is unlikely to be paying much attention, than with an older child. Furthermore, a one-year-old is going to be very accepting of whatever his parents say; a baby is not going to ask any tough questions or have a strong emotional reaction to the facts of his adoption. Those of us fortunate enough to have these early practice years can develop confidence in our ability to handle the subject. We'll need that confidence later on when the child does respond to talks about adoption with difficult questions and intense emotions.

Controversy over early discussion of adoption

Most of the parents I talk to intend to tell their children early that they are adopted. But not everyone agrees that it's wise to tell an infant or toddler that he is adopted. Because most children will not be able to comprehend what it really means to be adopted until about the age of five, some psychologists recommend waiting until then to tell children they are adopted. These psychologists are concerned that because the child doesn't know what being adopted means, he will see it as something that makes him different from other children and develop a negative self-image as a result.

I don't think that's a serious risk if parents are careful to talk about adoption as a *way of joining a family* rather than as a description of a person.

If adoption isn't discussed early in the child's life by his parents, not only is it likely that the child will be told or allowed to believe a lie, he may be told the truth by someone outside the family. Children should first hear about being adopted in a loving way from their parents.

And, of course, if this opportunity is missed, there's the risk that parents might find it easier to perpetuate the early deception and put off telling the child of his adoption indefinitely. (This possibility is explored further in Chapter 8.)

Finding natural opportunities

In looking for natural opportunities to talk about adoption with an infant we should pay attention to the times when we feel warm and loving about having the child. For example, when rocking a baby to sleep we might tell him the story of how he joined our family. Or when looking through a family photo album, we could point to a picture and say, "That's the day you came home from your foster family." When going through a box of mementos, we could say, "Here's the teddy bear your birthmother gave you when she said good-bye to you."

It may seem difficult at first to find natural opportunities to talk to an infant or toddler about his adoption through donor insemination or *in vitro* fertilization with a donor egg or embryo because he was born to the parents who are raising him. But there are occasions in which mentioning the child's birth story would be logical. For example, when driving past the fertility clinic, a parent might say, "That's where the doctor works who found a birthfather to help us make a baby."

In each of these instances, we are telling our child a crucial fact about being adopted: "There are other people who played significant roles in your life." Photographs in an album and special keepsakes are ways of showing the child that these people and the time he may have spent with them are important. And he's learning these facts in an atmosphere of love and caring.

Sometimes, in a well-meant effort to accustom a child to thinking of himself as adopted so he "always knows," a parent may say, "Where's my little adopted girl?" or "What a handsome little adopted boy!" But while it is natural to say to your child, "What a handsome little boy!" it isn't natural to say, "What a handsome little adopted boy!" By hearing about adoption in such artificial contexts, even young children can pick up the idea that adoption is something that makes them different from other children, when it is the way they joined their families that is different.

While eventually they will learn that because of their adoption, they have issues and perhaps expectations to deal with that other children do not have, we hope they will not think of adoption as something that makes them inferior.

An adoption vocabulary

Although an infant or toddler probably won't notice the words you use when you talk about adoption, it is important to get into the habit of using terms that convey a positive attitude about adoption and about the people involved in the adoption. I think we can become too sensitive about language, but the words we use to describe people and processes often reveal attitudes toward those people and processes.

Over the years, adoptive parents, adoptees, birthparents, and professionals have discussed which terms are preferable to use in describing traditional adoption, arriving at general agreement but certainly not consensus. The language used in adoption through donor insemination and *in vitro* fertilization is in the process of being examined.

Naturally, parents have to feel comfortable with the terms they use, and the important point is that children hear about adoption in a way that is positive without being sugar-coated.

Adoptees

Children shouldn't be labeled as "adopted." While I use the term "adopted child" or "adoptee" in writing about adoption to clarify who is being talked about, we should never differentiate between our children by the process by which they joined our family. Saying, "This is our adopted son Michael," is as inappropriate as, "This is our son Michael. He was conceived in a petri dish." Some people believe that even in writing, it is inappropriate to call someone an "adoptee" or "adopted child." They prefer to say "a child who has been adopted." I find that too cumbersome.

Individuals adopted through donor insemination sometimes refer to themselves as "donor offspring." Elizabeth Noble, in her book *Having Your Baby by Donor Insemination* (Boston: Houghton Mifflin Company, 1987), refers to them as DI children. Both of these strike me as awkward and clinical, and "donor offspring" seems to acknowledge only the father's role in the conception. We should acknowledge that children conceived through donor insemination share many issues with those who are adopted in a traditional way, and refer to them as "adopted through donor insemination." Children conceived by a surrogate mother are "adopted through surrogacy," and those conceived as a result of *in vitro* fertilization with a donor egg or donor embryo are "adopted through *in vitro* fertilization."

Biologic relatives

The terms "mother," "father," and "parents" appropriately belong to the child's legal parents. Therefore, adoptive parents should be called the child's "mother" and "father" rather than "adoptive mother" or "adoptive father." But again, in writing about various members of a child's family, I find it helpful to clarify which parents I'm referring to by using the adjective "adoptive." Similarly, there is no need to identify the child's grandparents, aunts, uncles, or other relatives as "adoptive."

I've heard individuals adopted through donor insemination refer to their adoptive fathers as their "social fathers." This is at best ambiguous.

When discussing the child's genetic parents, the terms

"birthmother" and "birthfather" or "biologic mother" and "biologic father" are generally accepted. If you adopted through surrogacy, the woman who gave birth to your child is the child's birthmother or biologic mother, and I think that is a more appropriate way to refer to her than as a surrogate mother.

Similarly, the man who donated the sperm that resulted in your child's conception is the child's birthfather or biologic father, although he is sometimes referred to by those adopted through donor insemination as the "donor father." The term "sperm donor" is too clinical and detached a way to refer to a child's biologic parent.

For children adopted traditionally or through donor insemination or surrogacy, the terms "biologic parents" and "birthparents" are interchangeable. But the biologic parent of a child adopted through *in vitro* fertilization will be different from his birthparent. The woman who donated the egg will be the child's biologic mother, while the woman who carried the child and gave birth to him will be his birthmother.

Biologic or birthparents are still called the "real mother" or "natural father" by those not sensitive to adoption issues, but many adoptive parents find these terms offensive. A few people believe terms describing parental roles should be reserved for the parents who actually raise the child. They prefer terms like "birth giver" to "birthmother."

In talking about the birthparents, keep in mind that a young child has difficulty understanding how the term "mother" can be used to describe the woman who gives birth as well as the woman who raises him. His mental development is not mature enough for him to understand what those two women have in common that justify their both being called his "mother." Consequently, he will be confused if he is told he has "two mothers – one who gave birth to him and one who is taking care of him." He needs different names for those two women. Although the words "birthmother" and "mother" share the same root, they are sufficiently different to satisfy a child's need to have different names for people with different functions, just as "grandmother" is sufficiently different from "mother" for a child to understand that they refer to people with different roles.

There are also situations in which it is appropriate to refer to the birthmother as a "woman," for example, instead of saying, "You grew inside another mother," say, "You grew inside another woman." It won't be until the child reaches an abstract level of thinking – usually after age eleven – that he can understand why his birthmother and his adoptive mother can both be called his "mother."

While I think it's important for a child to know the terms "birthmother" and "biologic father," and to whom they refer, if you have an open adoption, it is appropriate for a child to address his birthparents as naturally as possible. Today, that would probably be by their first names.

The family-building process

In describing the adoption process, parents can use the phrase "placed the child for adoption" to imply that the birthparents made a voluntary decision and a positive plan. While terms like "surrendered," "relinquished," and "given up for adoption" are so frequently used that they rise to our lips automatically, they can convey a negative decision to the child because they sound as though the child was snatched away from the birthparents against their wishes. When an unmarried woman has few options for an unplanned pregnancy, as women did years ago and do today in some countries, it may be accurate to say she "surrendered" her child. But in the United States today, birthmothers generally have more control over their decisions. Another common term, "adopted out," carries no sense of destination. "Put up for adoption" came into use at the turn of the century when orphan trains carried children to the Midwest where they were "put up" on platforms so they could be chosen by families.

Of course, the phrase "placed the child for adoption" is not accurate in all situations. In a stepparent adoption, saying the birthparent "made an adoption plan" also communicates a deliberate, orderly decision made with the welfare of the child in mind. The phrase "transferred his parental rights" is an accurate and acceptable term, but because children don't understand the legal system that governs adoption until they are about eleven years old, young children will not understand what it means to terminate or transfer parental rights.

The term "involuntary termination of parental rights" is used when the biologic parents' rights to their child are terminated against their wishes, but this is a phrase children will have difficulty understanding. Pediatrician Vera Fahlberg suggests that parents explain to their child that his birthparents didn't know how to ask for help in raising him, but that they gave some signals that they wanted help. Other people saw that the child was placed with parents who could nurture him as he needed and deserved.

In an effort to portray adoption as a positive experience, adoptive parents sometimes tell their children they were "chosen." While those who adopt older children often do select them from loose-leaf books filled with photographs and biographies of waiting children, most parents who adopt infants do not have a choice, so the term is often not accurate. More importantly, telling a child he was "chosen" implies that there are certain expectations of him that he must live up to if he is to remain "chosen." Thus a term that is meant to make a child feel secure in his family often has the opposite effect.

Like telling a child he was "chosen," telling him he is "special" because he is adopted is an attempt to make him feel good about his adoption because we expect him to feel bad. If we really believe that adoption is not a second-best way of forming a family we won't feel compelled to overcompensate for it by making it sound like it's really better to be adopted than to be born into a family. It's better to tell a child, "So, we decided to adopt a child, and we're glad that child was you."

In recent years, the term "donor insemination" has replaced the term "artificial insemination by donor." One reason is that the commonly used acronym for artificial insemination by donor, AID, became confused with the acronym for acquired immune deficiency syndrome, AIDS. A more compelling reason to change the name, however, is that "artificial insemination" conveys the idea that children are created artificially. "Donor insemination" conveys a somewhat more personal process.

Racial and ethnic references

We should describe racial or ethnic groups by their heritage and culture rather than by the skin color of those in the group. This point is made by John E. Williams and J. Kenneth Morland in their book *Race, Color, and the Young Child* (Chapel Hill, N.C.: University of North Carolina Press, 1976). Williams and Morland suggest that substituting Euro-American for white and African-American for black is more accurate, since nobody's skin is truly black, white, red, or yellow, but some shade of brown. Furthermore, terms such as Asian-American and Latin American acknowledge racial differences while pointing out that some culture is shared. Minority group leaders in the United States have recently endorsed this idea.

As we discuss in Chapter 3, the terms "biracial" and "mixed race" are meaningless terms in our society. Refer to your child by the racial or ethnic term that will apply to him based on his physical appearance.

Beginning the adoption story

For most children three years old and younger, brief and appropriate references to their adoption or to their birthparents are sufficient. Such references provide children with an awareness of adoption and establish an atmosphere of openness in the family. But some parents may want to tell a more complete story of how their children joined their families. Although children really won't understand a more detailed story, telling the story does give parents an opportunity to practice talking about adoption, and ensures that when children are ready for more information, the parents are ready with it.

When your child is an infant or toddler, if you choose to go beyond statements such as, "I'm so glad you came to live with us," or "Why don't we send this picture of you to your birthmother," keep the story simple but accurate, and take into account details about your child's story that will be added later as he matures mentally and emotionally. You might say something like:

> "Mommy and daddy wanted a baby very much, but couldn't make one themselves. You were made by another man and woman and you grew inside that other woman and were born to her just like other children are. Those people are called your birthmother and birthfather.
>
> But your birthmother and birthfather couldn't take care of a baby, so after you were born, you came to live with us. I'm sure they were sad that they were separated from you. You were probably sad, too, although you don't remember that. I was sad that you weren't born to me, but now we're happy that we're a family."

With this simple story, you've introduced the significant people in the child's life and some important elements of the full adoption story that you can build on later:

- You've identified your motives for adopting. It's important that the child realize you had needs, too, that were met by the adoption; it wasn't done as a charitable act.

- You've acknowledged the important role both birthparents had in the creation of your child and have presented them in a realistic but empathetic way.

• By saying the birthparents "couldn't take care of a baby," you've suggested why the birthparents decided to place the child for adoption in a way that places responsibility for the decision on them, and not the child. That is, they had a problem—they weren't able to care for *a baby*. There wasn't anything about the child that made him more difficult to care for than other babies. This will be more important later on when the child realizes that most children are not placed for adoption and wonders if it happened to him because there was something wrong with him.

• You've let the child know that he was conceived, grew inside his birthmother, and was born just as all children are. This will be more important later on when the child better understands reproduction.

• You've acknowledged that there are feelings associated with adoption and that some of them are good feelings and some of them are sad or angry feelings.

This story is basic enough that it will fit a variety of adoption scenarios, including the birthmother who abandons her child, the birthparent whose parental rights were terminated as a result of abuse, and the child conceived as a result of rape or incest.

With a few alterations, the story will also fit other adoption circumstances:

Open adoption

The term "open adoption" refers to a wide variety of adoption practices ranging from adoptions in which adoptive parents and birthparents share nonidentifying information about themselves, such as their occupations or first names, to those in which the two sets of parents agree to have ongoing contact with each other, including visits with the child.

If a child is going to have contact with his birthparents, he should not be misled as to who those people are. It is difficult to talk to a very young child about the complexities of adoption, but in the long run, it's easier to start with the truth and build on it than it is to keep track of the story you've made up, tell the child the real story when you've determined he is old enough, and explain why you lied to him. Furthermore, by telling the truth right from the start, you won't have to worry about someone else telling the child.

> "Mommy and daddy wanted a baby very much, but couldn't make one themselves. You were made by another man and woman and you grew inside that other woman. That other woman is Patti, and she is your birthmother. But Patti and your birthfather couldn't take care of a baby, so you came to live with us. They were sad that they couldn't take care of a baby. You were probably sad, too, although you don't remember that. I was sad that you weren't born to me, but now we're happy that we're a family. Patti likes to see you because she cares about you and wants to see that you are happy and that you're growing big and strong."

Donor insemination and <u>in</u> <u>vitro</u> fertilization with a donor egg or embryo

"Mommy and daddy wanted a baby very much, but it isn't always easy for a mommy and daddy to make a baby. Daddy's body (or 'Mommy's body,' or 'Daddy's and Mommy's bodies') wasn't working right, so another man (or 'woman' or 'man and woman') helped make you grow inside mommy."

Young children do not understand reproduction or reproductive technology well enough to understand donor insemination or *in vitro* fertilization. But parents who are concerned that a child might be led to believe his mother engaged in extramarital sex might want to add, "Mommy never met your biologic father. The doctor put sperm from your biologic father inside mommy so a baby would grow. And that baby was you."

You can also add: "Mommy and daddy were sad that daddy (or mommy) couldn't help make you, and your biologic father (or biologic mother) is probably sad sometimes that he (she) never got a chance to meet you, but I'm happy that you could grow inside mommy and we're all happy that we're a family."

Families with adopted and biologic children

"After Jason and Peter were born, mommy and daddy thought they were all the children we would have in our family. But as Jason and Peter got older, we kept thinking it would be nice to have some more children. But we didn't want to make another baby. ('Mommy was getting too old to make a baby,' or 'We wanted our next child to be about the same age as Jason and Peter − a baby would have been too young,' or 'We wanted to be sure the next child would be a girl.')"

Because a biologic child could have been possible, it is important to acknowledge that you benefited from the adoption so that the child doesn't think he is expected to feel grateful to you for adopting instead of giving birth. Even though you may have been motivated by a commitment to zero population growth, adoption was not a sacrifice for you−you needed something, too, that adoption satisfied. Often that need is as simple as a need to nurture children.

If a child was adopted as a result of infertility experienced by the parents after the birth of a biologic child, parents can explain that sometimes parents' bodies work right for a while, then stop working right, and that is what happened to them.

Stepparent adoption

"Before you were born, I was married to (or 'living with' or 'in love with') another man. Together, he and I made you, and you grew inside me and were born. Then we decided we didn't want to be together any more, and we had to decide whether you would live with me or with him. We decided I should take care of you.

After a while, I fell in love with daddy and we decided to get married. When we got married, daddy started to help me take care of you and soon he loved you and you loved him. And he decided he wanted everyone to know he was your daddy. We wanted to ask your birthfather if that was all right, but I didn't know where he lived any more, so we couldn't ask him. Your birthfather was sad when we couldn't be a family any more, but I'll bet he'd be happy to know you have a daddy who is with you all the time."

Single parent adoption

"Mommy wanted a child very much, but it takes a mommy and a daddy to make a baby and I didn't have a husband..."

The single parent would probably explain the rest of the adoption story as would a parent in a two-parent family.

Gay and lesbian parenthood

Gay men and lesbians who choose to adopt a child explain their motivation much the way any single parent who adopts would. A young child does not need to know why there is no man or woman in his parent's life. Those who adopt through donor insemination should acknowledge that the child has a father, but needn't explain at this time why that method of adoption was used. The parent who arranged for her own donor insemination could say, for example:

"I wanted a baby very much. Your birthfather knew how much I wanted a baby, and even though we both knew that it wasn't going to be possible for us all to live together as a family, he said he would be your father."

There apparently are few resources available for gay and lesbian parents to use in explaining their lifestyle to their children. *River of Promise: Two Women's Story of Love and Adoption*, by Judy Dahl (Available from LuraMedia, P.O. Box 261668, 10227 Autumnview Lane, San Diego, Calif. 92126-0998) is a touching story of the adoption of two infants by a lesbian couple. *Rocking the Cradle: Lesbian Mothers: A Challenge in Family Living*, by Gillian E. Hanscombe and Jackie Forster (Boston: Alyson Publications, 1982), describes the social and personal implications of lesbian motherhood. The Lesbians Choosing Children Network (46 Pleasant Street, Cambridge, Mass. 02139) was unable to refer me to any children's literature on gay and lesbian lifestyles, but they may be aware of such books as they become available.

Adoption via surrogacy

"Mommy and daddy wanted a baby very much, but mommy's body wasn't working properly, so she couldn't make a baby. Mommy and daddy decided to ask another woman whose body was working just fine if she would help us have a baby. She already had two children that she loved very much, and she was sad that we couldn't make a baby, so she said she would help us. Daddy's body was working okay, so he helped make you, and you grew inside that other woman, who is called your birthmother. When you were born, you came to live with us. I was sad that you didn't grow inside me, but now we're happy that we're a family."

Balancing discussion of adoption

"I was telling my child his adoption story and as soon as I

had finished it, he jumped off my lap and began playing with his blocks," one mother told me. "He just didn't seem to be interested."

Parents sometimes tell me they're concerned that they will talk about adoption too much and their children will feel strange because they are adopted.

Extremes are rarely good. It is possible to talk about adoption too much just as it is possible to talk about it too little. You may not be able to judge this solely by the feedback you receive from your child. Young children have short attention spans. Just because a toddler jumps off his mother's lap after his adoption story is told doesn't mean he wasn't interested in it, although it is a good clue that he doesn't want to hear any more at that time. Just because he doesn't have any apparent reaction to what was said doesn't mean he wasn't interested or didn't gain anything from the interaction. If your child jumped off your lap after a discussion of why he shouldn't talk to strangers, would you decide that since he didn't seem interested, you wouldn't talk about it any more? Of course not. You'd probably hope that he picked up some information, and you'd recognize that this is a complicated topic that you would need to discuss again. However, you might decide to pick a different time or setting for the next discussion.

A better clue to whether you are discussing adoption excessively is your own assessment of the situation. Did you feel you had to seek out an opportunity to discuss adoption? Was it awkward to begin? Did your son jump down to play with blocks because you had interrupted his play to initiate the discussion? If you are seizing or creating natural opportunities rather than artificial ones to discuss adoption, you probably aren't discussing adoption excessively.

Just because adoption is an important topic, discussions needn't always be intense, serious "on-the-lap-in-the-rocking-chair" kinds of interactions. Indeed, if you are handling adoption in a matter-of-fact way, you'll find yourself talking about it briefly while you are cooking dinner, driving in the car, and doing other routine activities. The length of time you talk about it will be appropriate to whatever aspect of adoption you are discussing. One parent said simply, "Did you know Superman was adopted, too?" when she saw her son watching a Superman cartoon.

You may be surprised to hear your toddler telling you or someone else his adoption story because you haven't expected him to fully understand it. In fact, he probably doesn't, but is simply repeating a story he's heard repeatedly.

Talking to others about adoption

While there may be few opportunities and little need for parents to talk about adoption with their children when they are infants or toddlers, the topic often comes up with relatives, friends, and even strangers.

Some of these encounters make us feel uncomfortable— even with members of our own family or close friends. It isn't unusual for people who do not have personal experience with adoption to use language or express attitudes that reflect the public perception of adoption as a second-best way of forming a family. When one couple I talked to decided to adopt, they decided to share the news with their family physician, who had earlier referred them to a fertility specialist. "We've decided to adopt," the wife told him. "I'm so sorry," he replied, focusing on the "failure" of medical science rather than the feelings of the prospective adoptive parents.

Furthermore, adoption often involves a court action, and therefore may be considered by some to be a public activity. Some people who wouldn't dream of commenting on an individual's private reproductive activities think little about commenting on more public ways of forming families.

Because adoption is so misunderstood by society, I believe all of us involved with adoption have a responsibility to be advocates for adoption—not in the sense of encouraging others to adopt, but by educating people about what adoption is really like.

Yet I also believe that information about a child's origins is private information belonging to that child. As parents of a minor child we act as guardians of that information, acting in what we think are the child's best interests.

Keeping private information private

Parents I talk to agree that children have a right to have their privacy protected, but they aren't always sure what information should be considered private.

As an adoptive parent, I'm quite willing to answer people's questions about the adoption process, the practices of different agencies, our reasons for adopting, and how my children reacted to what was a major change in their lives.

I consider information to be "private" if it refers to a child's genetic and social history – who their parents were, what they were like, why they placed the child for adoption, and actual or possible medical conditions the child might have. If you are unsure about whether or not to share something, think about whether you would readily share that information about yourself. Would you want people to know you had an alcoholic father? That there was a risk of congenital syphilis when you were born? That you were so poorly cared for by your mother that you had oozing sores all over your body?

Another rule of thumb is to never share information that you plan to keep from your child until he is much older. Aside from the philosophical problem involved with that, there is a possibility of your child learning something unpleasant about himself from someone else, and realizing that while you kept it from him, you shared it with the world.

While parents generally understand that they should not, for example, tell acquaintances their child had been sexually abused by her birthfather, they are not quite so sure what should be shared with members of their extended families.

In most cases, even close relatives do not have to know the child's history to understand the child's behavior. It is possible to say, "I don't want to go into all the details, because I think it should be Kelly's choice when she's older whether or not to talk about what happened before she joined our family. But it is important for you to know that she is uncomfortable when men hug or kiss her, so until she gets to know you and indicates she's ready for physical affection, please try to show your affection in other ways."

Even if you are implying information about the child's origins rather than sharing it outright, make sure others know that you expect them to keep the information confidential, and make sure you agree on what confidential means.

When a casual acquaintance or stranger asks a question that is too personal, parents can respond with an answer that educates people but does not reveal private information about their child or family. For example:

Friend: "I've heard a lot of these children arrive covered with parasites. Was Rachel?"

Parent: "I remember being concerned about that. Actually, I don't think as many children have problems with that as we're led to believe. But the agencies want parents to be prepared for the absolute worst."

Friend: "How much do you know about her real parents?"

Parent: "You mean her birthparents? Actually, we're quite satisfied with what we've been told."

Most people will realize that you don't care to provide more information but not be offended by your answers. Those who persist are usually discouraged by a polite, but firm, "I appreciate your interest, but I think that information is private information that belongs to Rachel, and it should be her decision whether or not to share it."

Parents may be reluctant to respond in such a cool way,

however, to a close friend, especially one who has shared with them the emotional highs and lows of infertility and the adoption process. To that person a parent can say something like, "If you were asking something about me I wouldn't hesitate to tell you, but one of the things that was really emphasized to us in the adoption process was that information like that belongs to the child and that we as parents have no right to share it with those outside the family."

There may be information about your child that a doctor or psychologist would need to know for the child's own well-being. Such professionals are accustomed to keeping information confidential, and I see no problem discussing your child's past with them.

However, before working with any professional, take the time to meet him and discuss adoption. There are some medical personnel and other professionals who have biases or misconceptions about adoption, and who consequently may make a remark in front of your child that they are unaware could be offensive or harmful. By assessing this possibility ahead of time, you can educate the individual or choose another professional.

(Talking with school personnel about your child is discussed in Chapter 5.)

Responding to relatives

Most of us who adopt do our families a disservice by expecting them to be completely supportive of our decision immediately. We forget that we may have struggled ourselves with questions about whether or not to adopt; what age of child to adopt; and what race, what sex, and what kinds of physical or emotional disabilities we could accept. We may have had questions about whether a surrogate contract was an appropriate way to build a family, the impact of donor insemination on the child's adoptive father, whether there was any mental illness or debilitating genetic disease in the child's biologic family, whether an open adoption would be confusing for the child, and more.

For example, when a grandparent says, as one parent told me her mother did, "She's a lovely baby. And maybe you'll still be able to have one of your own," remember that before we could add this child to our family, we had to grieve for the fantasy child that this child or any child would never be. This grandparent, and other family members, may have fantasies about our children that they have not yet let go of.

So we should give our families time to adjust to the idea of adoption, provide them with information that will help them understand our decision, give them an opportunity to express their feelings and have those feelings respected rather than challenged, and finally, forgive them for anything negative they might say or do while they adjust to the way we chose to form our families. It's often helpful to provide them with a neutral environment in which to learn about adoption and express their feelings. Many adoption agencies, adoptive parent organizations, and chapters of Resolve, Inc., an infertility information and support group, offer adoption education classes or conferences either expressly designed for relatives of adoptive parents or suitable for them. You can also select reading material that you think will help them understand adoption.

Given an opportunity to understand your decision, work through their own feelings, and observe that the decision you've made is right for you, most family members come to accept adoption and love the children that come into the family. When they don't, or when, despite their love for your children, they discuss adoption inappropriately, it can be disturbing.

If after several years and many second chances, a relative still won't accept an adopted child as a complete member of the family, parents can choose to sever contact with that relative or accept that contact with them will always be unsatisfactory. But parents can demand that the relative be respectful toward the child in his presence. When anyone discusses adoption inappropriately, regardless of whether they are eight years old or eighty-eight, they should be told that their remark was inappropriate, and the child should know that his parents are taking care of the situation. How this is done depends on the parent's relationship with the relative making the remark and his instinct about the most effective approach. It may be a gentle reminder, a humorous comment, or an exclamation of amazement or outrage. While the individual shouldn't be embarrassed, parents do have a responsibility to speak up for the child who potentially is hurt by such comments and to let that child know they are doing so. Some parents might talk to the relative in front of the child, while others would choose to take the child aside and say, "Grandpa shouldn't have said that. I'll talk to him later when there aren't a lot of people around."

Responding to inappropriate remarks

Sometimes someone asks a question about our children that doesn't involve private information, but is nonetheless intrusive or reflects a negative attitude toward adoption that we are tired of confronting.

This can be a tricky situation. Most of us want to respond politely to people. We want to educate those who are ignorant of adoption or sincere about wanting to learn more about it. We want to convey that we are comfortable with adoption; it isn't something we are too ashamed to talk about.

Many parents "give in" and answer the question because to do otherwise would involve being more assertive than we feel comfortable being. But my own experience, and that of parents I've talked to, is that we're angry with ourselves when we respond politely to questions about our families that we really don't want to answer.

For example, parents sometimes tell me they don't know what to say when someone incorrectly assumes their child is biologically related to both parents. Some parents correct the person or allow them to believe the falsehood, depending on how well they know the person asking, whether the parents will ever have any further contact with the person asking, the attitude expressed when making the remark, the parent's feelings at the time, and whether the child is present and able to understand the discussion. To someone who says, "He must look like his father" (a favorite comment of those who have adopted transracially), parents sometimes respond, "Yes, he does," or "Probably, but he's adopted so I don't know for sure." In the case of donor insemination parents might want to say something like, "He probably looks like his biologic father but he has a lot of his father's mannerisms." One woman, who was distracted when she was asked that question, unthinkingly replied, "I don't know. I don't know who his father is."

If you choose to respond in a way that allows people to believe something other than the truth, be sure that you explain to your child why you made that decision. You can say, "The information that person was asking was none of her business, so I didn't give it to her." Even though a very young child or infant is probably not going to comprehend the discussion that took place or the parent's response, clarification is a good habit to get into.

Those families in which there is a mix of children from different parents often find themselves forced to identify their children by their parentage. "Which is the adopted one?" or "Which ones are *yours*?" are offensive questions because they imply that your relationship with your children is different depending on how they joined your family. One parent told me she tried to convey the inappropriateness of the question without being rude by feigning confusion – glancing quickly from one child to the next in an obvious effort to "remember" which one is adopted. Many parents say they embrace all their children and say, "They're all mine." In such situations, responding "Why do you ask?" forces the individual to confront her own motives and prejudices. If the individual then responds, "I was wondering because my husband and I are thinking about adopting," you can proceed to address her real questions about adoption. If, as it more likely will be, the individual says, "I was just curious," you can reply, "Oh," and leave the discussion at that, hoping the person will recognize the inappropriateness of the question once you have (politely) challenged her reason for asking it and chosen not to respond.

Parents tell me the most disturbing question they are asked is: "Are they really brother and sister?" While some people may be genuinely interested in whether you have adopted a sibling group, the question is irritating because it implies that the relationship between your children is somehow going to be different because they do not have the same birthparents. While any number of flip replies may spring to your lips when someone asks you this question, the best reply may again be: "You mean are they related biologically? Why do you ask?" If the person replies that they are thinking about adopting a sibling group, you might say, "If you want to find out more about that, let me suggest that you call some friends of mine who have more experience with that than I do." If the reply is, "I was wondering because they look so much alike," you can respond, "Do you really think so?"

Questions like these are most likely to be asked by someone who doesn't know your family well enough to already know the answers. But sometimes a close friend whom you haven't seen recently, fellow church member, or co-worker will ask a question, and you will want to be more responsive.

I remember when a friend heard me reprimand my daughter and said to me, "You sound like a real mother." I was too surprised then to do anything but smile weakly. Today I might put my hands on my hips and say humorously, "I have spent the past six weeks getting up in the middle of every *real* night trying to *really* toilet train this *real* child. Of course I sound like a *real* mother."

Another parent might say, "I'm sure you didn't mean to hurt me, but I feel like this child's real mother, and she feels like I'm her real mother, and it sounds like you doubt that."

Nonadopted children and siblings

Keep in mind that as with the child who is adopted, the ability of other children to understand aspects of adoption will change with their developmental progress. A single explanation of why you are adopting will not suffice for them any more than it will suffice for the child who is adopted. In talking once with a group of pre-adolescent children, all of whom had been born into their families and who had siblings who were adopted, I was surprised that none of them could tell me why their parents had decided to adopt. One said her parents decided to adopt because they had all girls and wanted a boy. "But then they adopted a girl!" she said. She had never learned why they had changed their minds. I suspect that in all these families the parents had explained their reasons for adopting, but the children didn't fully comprehend the explanations at the time.

Private information about a child's origins should not be shared with siblings any more than they should be shared with those outside the family because in most cases, siblings can't be trusted to keep such "secrets." Like other people, siblings can be told, "That information belongs to Jeremy. When he's older, he can decide if he wants you to know about it."

If there is private information that can't be kept from the siblings, for example, if the child is a hepatitis B carrier, they need to be helped to understand why it is important for that information to remain private. For example, you can say, "Most people don't know a lot about hepatitis B and they are scared of people who are hepatitis B carriers. We know that hepatitis B isn't spread by casual contact. So as long as Pam behaves the way we've talked about, there is no need for other people to know that she is a carrier."

If children need information about a sibling for their own protection, it is sufficient to discuss the child's current problem. The siblings do not need to know why the child has that problem. For example, a parent can say: "Before Jack came to live with us, he learned some ways to behave that we don't allow in this family. So he might want to touch you or have you touch him in an inappropriate way. I want you to know this so that you aren't surprised if he makes such suggestions and are ready with ways to tell him 'no.' And I want you to let daddy and me know if he makes such suggestions. You won't get into trouble, and we won't let Jack hurt you for telling us."

Siblings of children who have been adopted need support just as parents do. While some parents wonder if they should "drag" their biologic children to picnics with the adoption organizations they belong to, it helps the siblings to know that there are other children who are faced with questions at school and feelings at home as a result of having an adopted brother or sister. (Families with both adopted and biologic children are discussed further in Chapter 5.)

If a child in your family is speaking unacceptably about a child who has just joined your family through adoption and gentle reminders of better ways to talk about adoption don't seem to be having any effect, it could be a sign the child is upset about the new child. One mother told me her twelve-year-old couldn't be happier about the adoption of an infant with Down Syndrome. But she was so happy she announced to everyone—shop clerks, waitresses, and strangers—that they had just adopted a baby with Down Syndrome. It could be that even though the girl loves the baby, she is a bit embarrassed at having a mentally retarded sister. She is perhaps confused by those seemingly contradictory feelings and may also be embarrassed to have them. So she covers up by acting happy in a way that lets everyone know that she isn't "really" related to this mentally retarded baby. Her parents might want to let her know that feeling embarrassed at having a mentally retarded sister is an honest emotion, saying, for example, "I wonder if you ever worry that people will make fun of you because your sister has Down Syndrome?" They could also provide her with an opportunity to express her feelings about her sister in a "safe" setting, for example, in a group of other siblings of adopted children or other siblings of children with Down Syndrome.

Often when families adopt a child, their friends and relatives see it as a chance to explain adoption to their children. When we adopted our first child, a close friend, whose children were three and six, told me that she was grateful for the opportunity to explain adoption to her children. However, parents can't assume that their friends and relatives, who probably have not attended adoption education classes or read adoption literature, will understand how to explain adoption sensitively or be prepared for the questions their children will ask.

While parents can't tutor every acquaintance in how to discuss adoption with children, they can volunteer information to family members with children or to close friends about how they intend to explain adoption to their child, and why they believe it is important to discuss adoption in these ways.

If the child who is adopted is of a different race or ethnic group than the rest of the family, the parents can explain to their relatives and friends that while they expect adults to refrain from making any derogatory remarks about minorities (see "The minority family" later in this chapter), pre-schoolers are expected to notice and comment on physical differences among people. They can say that such comments should be responded to matter-of-factly and nonjudgmentally, so that the child learns that while there are physical differences, they don't make the child better or worse than anyone else.

Introducing the child's heritage

Parents who adopt children of different racial or ethnic backgrounds have a responsibility to acquaint their children with their heritage and help them feel proud to be a member of that group.

Before your child understands that he's adopted, he'll

understand that he is African–American, Latin American, Native American, East Indian–American, Asian–American, Euro–American, or a member of some other group. And before he understands that he is different from other children because he is adopted, he'll be aware that his race makes him different from other people. (The development of racial awareness is discussed in Chapter 3.) Because children are aware of people's skin color by the age of three and are aware that they are a member of a particular racial group by the time they are four, it's never too early to introduce them to their heritage. This can't be done in a didactic way; it must be done by incorporating aspects of the child's heritage into your family life. In that way, you say to the child, "Our family is a mixture of our heritage and yours." Thus, while it's nice to have travel posters of the child's country of origin in his room, or samples of ceremonial clothing packed away with other special mementos, it's more important to find ways of adding parts of your child's heritage to your way of life. For example, you may want to make celebrating Martin Luther King's birthday as important in your family as celebrating the Fourth of July.

After learning that in Korea, particular rituals are used to celebrate a child's first birthday, my husband and I decided to incorporate some of these into our children's birthday celebrations. They delivered rice cakes to the neighbors and chose their "fortune" from a tray filled with pencils, coins, and thread. While they did not understand the significance of those activities at the time, as they've grown older, the photographs of their first birthday parties have provided us with opportunities to discuss their Korean heritage and have been another way they've learned that we have considered their culture to be an important part of our family life.

While their children are young, parents can sample the foods of the child's country of origin or ethnic group and decide which ones their family likes well enough to be made a part of their repertoire of regular meals. Parents can also become knowledgeable enough about their child's racial or ethnic group to be able to provide him with cultural information in a routine way. For example, if a family was preparing to attend a wedding, parents could describe how a wedding would be handled if the child was with his birth family.

It isn't difficult to find books outlining the customs, folk tales, histories, and cultural contributions of different racial and ethnic groups. (See Adoptive Families of America in Appendix A: "Do We Need More Help?") By familiarizing yourselves with these when your child is very young, you can decide when and how to incorporate them into family life.

The minority family

If your child is a member of a minority, he not only should feel proud to be Native American or Mexican–American, he should feel comfortable being part of a minority. He not only should be knowledgeable about his heritage, he should know how to handle discrimination when it arises.

Teasing on the basis of differences, including racial differences, generally begins around the time children enter school (see "When children tease" in Chapter 5). Before that time, however, Euro–American parents can start thinking of themselves as a minority family, rather than as a Euro–American family with African–American or Asian–American children. You have been stared at by strangers because you are a minority family just as your child will be stared at because he is a member of a minority.

This fact was made clear to a family who had been invited to spend a weekend with friends at a lakeside cabin near an area in which white supremacists had recently been active. Not until they were at the cabin did they realize that their entire family was at risk from white supremacists – not just their Asian–American child. They returned from an uneasy weekend determined to be more conscious of themselves as a minority family.

While your child is young, incorporate into your family life aspects of many different cultures, not just that of your child's family of origin. By reading books illustrated with children of different racial groups, buying dolls of different races, and playing music from around the world, you say to your child, "In this family we value the contributions all peoples have made to the world." When your child reaches the school-age years and begins to experience discrimination personally, this will be an important foundation to have laid. (See "Racial and ethnic awareness" in Chapter 5.)

It's also necessary to make a conscious effort to eliminate any expression of prejudice or stereotyping from your lives and not to tolerate it in those around you. If you adopt an African–American child, for example, you will no doubt be sensitive to racial comments about African–American people. But it's also important to be sensitive to comments about other groups. If Polish jokes or unkind remarks about blind people are still tolerated, that tells a child, "It's okay to make fun of people because they are different." While your child is still young, become sensitive to any vestiges of prejudice in your life. While you may not be able to change your feelings, you can make a concerted effort to eliminate any expression of those feelings. Don't forget to pay attention to nonverbal messages about minorities. Children acquire positive and negative feelings about different minority groups through overheard conversations, by observing the behavior of people, through television and children's books, and in other informal ways. For example, if you act suspicious when an African–American person is seen walking in your Euro–American neighborhood, that tells your child, "African–Americans aren't to be trusted," and "African–Americans don't belong in our neighborhood." Furthermore, get in the habit of telling people who make derogatory comments or jokes about minority groups that as a minority family you are offended by such statements. You can't protect your child from all prejudicial statements, but you can let him know that you don't share them and don't tolerate those who do. One parent found it necessary to explain to his mother that her derogatory remarks about African–Americans was offensive to him as part of a minority family, even though his children were Latin American.

Eventually, you will want to talk with your child about his race, his ethnic heritage, religious background, or other minority distinction. In these early years, however, parents must be aware of the attitudes that are conveyed through their verbal and nonverbal communication.

Activity: Making an adoption story book

The most common request I receive is: "What books do you recommend using to explain adoption to a young child?" While there are many books for children about traditional adoption (see Appendix B: "Bibliography of Children's Books"), there are few books for children yet that discuss less common kinds of adoption such as single parent adoption, or adoption through donor insemination, surrogacy, or *in vitro* fertilization. Some of the books that are available suffer from the lack of an interesting plot and interesting characters. And because every adoption is just a little bit different, it's unlikely that any of them will describe precisely what took place in your family.

The best story book to use in talking to your child about adoption is one you make yourself that describes your child and your adoption experience just the way it really happened. You don't have to be an artist or author to tell the story of how your child joined your family. Get some marking pens, colored pencils, or crayons and some plain white paper. You could also use one of the commercially available computer programs for designing children's books. It's helpful to write the story first, usually limiting yourself to one statement on each page. Be sure to tell what was happening to you as well as what was happening to the child. Then go back and illustrate each statement. If you prefer, you can use photographs instead of drawings, but don't worry about your drawings not being of professional quality. Little details like making your house the right color is enough for a child to recognize that it is "his" house.

One child's adoption story might go something like this:

Page 1: "Once upon a time there was a man named Jack and a woman named Hannah.

Page 2: "They lived in a white house in Anytown, U.S.A.

Page 3: "Jack built houses.

Page 4: "Hannah was a lawyer, so she worked in the courthouse.

Page 5: "When they weren't working, Jack liked to play the piano.

Page 6: "And Hannah liked to play racquetball.

Page 7: "They were very happy except for one thing.

Page 8: "They wanted a baby, but they weren't able to make one themselves.

Page 9: "They wrote letters to lots of doctors that said, 'If you know of a woman who can't take care of a baby, please tell her that we would like to be that baby's parents.'

Page 10: "One day they got a call from a doctor who said he had showed their letter to a woman who wanted to find parents to take care of her baby.

Page 11: "The doctor said the woman wanted to meet Jack and Hannah to find out if they would make good parents for her baby.

Page 12: "So Jack and Hannah got on a plane and flew to Anothertown, U.S.A. to meet the mother.

Page 13: "They liked her right away, and she liked them.

Page 14: "The woman told them she was sad that she wasn't able to take care of a baby, but she could tell that Jack and Hannah would love her baby very much.

Page 15: "She told them when the baby was born, Jack and Hannah could take the baby home and be the baby's parents.

Page 16: "Jack and Hannah told her they would write her letters and send her pictures so that she would know how her baby was doing.

Page 17: "The woman said she would write letters, too.

Page 18: "Jack and Hannah flew home and waited for the day their baby would be born.

Page 19: "On March 25, 1989 they got a phone call from the doctor.

Page 20: " 'You have a baby girl,' he told them.

Page 21: "The next day Jack and Hannah flew back to Anothertown, U.S.A.

Page 22: "They went to the hospital where their baby was born.

Page 23: "The baby's birthmother gave her to Hannah. Everybody cried—even the baby.

Page 24: " 'What are you going to name her?' the birthmother asked.

Page 25: " 'We're going to call her Lisa,' Jack said.

Page 26: "The next day Jack and Hannah and Lisa flew back to Anytown, happy that they are now a family.

Page 27: "When they got home they found that their friends had decorated their house with balloons and a sign that said 'Welcome home, Lisa.' "

Put the illustrated pages in a photo album or three-ring binder with plastic-covered pages and you will have a story that your child will want to hear over and over again, and that you will enjoy reading to him.

3. "Where Did I Come From?"

The Preschool Years

Four-year-olds are known for their unending questions, especially those starting with "Why." This questioning comes from a genuine curiosity about the world they live in – a world that is expanding for them as they become more independent and move increasingly into the community. Their questioning also reflects their expanding mental ability. They can now comprehend time and space, which means they can consider experiences and places outside of present reality, such as past Christmas celebrations and the house where Grandma lives. So it's only natural that preschoolers start to have "life and death" kinds of questions. Where did all these things on earth – plants, cars, rabbits, and people – come from? And where will they all go when they die? And because the pre-school child is still primarily concerned with herself, she wants to know where *she* came from.

Talking about your child's birth will naturally lead to talking about her adoption. In these conversations you may repeat much of what you told your child when she was an infant or toddler because the meaning of how she was conceived, born, and joined your family now is more comprehensible to her. (Examples of how to introduce adoption to a toddler were given in Chapter 2.)

Four-, five-, and six-year-olds should be gaining an understanding of how they joined their families and developing good feelings about it. Now that the child is beginning to develop an awareness of what adoption really means, it is even more important for parents to convey that they are comfortable talking about the subject.

Talking about where babies come from

Preschoolers are primarily concerned with the immediate pasts of babies – how they grew inside their mothers and were born. They are less concerned with how babies are conceived. As a result, they are more interested in the mother's role than the father's. Nevertheless, it's generally best to start at the beginning, recognizing that the discussion of conception need only be brief and simple at this point. (Sex education books directed at preschoolers are listed in Appendix B: "Bibliography of Children's Books.")

Child: "How does the baby get inside the mommy?"

Parent: "It takes a father and a mother to make a baby. All babies start when a sperm from a man joins with an egg from a woman. Usually the sperm joins the egg inside the woman's body, but even when the sperm and egg are joined outside the woman and then placed in her body, all babies grow inside a woman's uterus and come out of a woman as a newborn baby.

"Not every man and woman can make a baby. Sometimes the man doesn't have enough sperm. Sometimes the woman's body doesn't work properly. When that happens, they may ask another man or woman to help them make a baby. Or, they may bring a baby into their family that was born to a man and woman who were unable to take care of a baby."

With this brief explanation, you establish that all babies result from the joining of an egg and a sperm, grow in a woman's body, and are born. You also introduce the idea that not all babies come from the father and mother they live with. (Although children are often told that a baby grows in a woman's tummy or stomach, I think it's important that children learn that a baby grows in a woman's uterus. It can be confusing for children to think that a stomach has more than one function. Furthermore, a child born to infertile parents may be troubled or confused by the idea that "mommy's tummy wasn't working properly.") Once your child has a basic understanding of conception, you can then explain more specifically how your child was conceived or joined your family.

Traditional adoption

"Mommy and daddy couldn't make a baby that would grow inside mommy. We knew that sometimes people who can make a baby aren't able to take care of a baby, so we talked to a woman who helps people out when they can't take care of a baby. She told us that because so many people want to adopt babies, we would have to wait a long time before there would be a baby for us. After a long time, we got a telephone call telling us that a baby had been born to a man and woman who couldn't take care of a baby. They wanted us to be that baby's father and mother. That baby was you."

Adoption through donor insemination

"Mommy and daddy couldn't make a baby that would grow inside mommy because daddy's body wasn't making sperm. The doctor took some sperm from another man and put it inside mommy where it joined with an egg from her body to make a baby. The baby grew inside her uterus and came out of her body when it was time to be born. That baby was you."

Adoption through surrogacy

"Mommy and daddy couldn't make a baby that would grow inside mommy because mommy's uterus didn't work the right way. The doctor took some sperm from daddy and placed it inside another woman where it joined with an egg from her body to make a baby. The baby grew inside her uterus and came out of her body when it was time to be born. That baby was you."

Adoption through <u>in vitro</u> fertilization with a donor egg or embryo

"Mommy and daddy couldn't make a baby that would grow inside mommy because mommy's body wasn't working right. So the doctor took an egg from another woman and mixed it with some sperm from daddy (or from another man). When it started to grow into a baby, the doctor put it inside mommy's uterus. The baby kept growing inside mommy and came out of her body when it was time to be born. That baby was you."

If a surrogate gestational mother was used, the story can be adapted to say the fertilized egg was placed inside "another woman" and after the baby was born, came to live with her adoptive parents.

Discussing intercourse

At some point the child will ask, or you may decide it is appropriate for the child to learn, how the sperm gets into the mother's body. A discussion of intercourse should begin with a discussion of male and female anatomy. You should explain that the motive for sexual intercourse is a desire to be close because the two people love each other very much. You should also explain that babies aren't made every time a man and woman have intercourse. Even if your child was conceived through sexual intercourse, you should explain that while sexual intercourse is the most common way babies are made, there are other ways for sperm and an egg to be joined:

Parent: "Do you remember when you got your shot? The doctor used a syringe to put a vaccine inside you so that you wouldn't get certain diseases. Sometimes the man's sperm is placed into a syringe and a doctor inserts the syringe into the woman's vagina."

Child: "Does it hurt? It hurt me when I got my shot."

Parent: "No, it doesn't hurt, because the doctor doesn't use a needle."

You would also want to explain *in vitro* fertilization:

Parent: "Sometimes the doctor takes an egg from the woman and mixes it in a glass dish with sperm from the man. When it looks like a baby has started growing, the doctor places the baby in the woman's uterus."

Child: "How does he get the baby inside the mother?"

Parent: "When a baby first starts to grow it is very, very tiny, so it's easy for the doctor to put it inside the woman's uterus."

Discussing birth

Keeping in mind that the child's major interest at this age is in how babies are *born* rather than conceived, don't neglect to discuss the birth of a baby.

Parent: "When it's time for the baby to be born, the mother gets some cramps in her uterus, which feel like a tummy ache or like you sometimes feel when you have to go to the bathroom. When that happens, the opening to her uterus begins to stretch so that it will be big enough for the baby to be born through. The mother pushes the baby out through her vagina."

Child: "Does it hurt?"

Parent: "It hurts a little bit, but a mother doesn't mind the pain because she is so happy that her baby is being born."

Children often like to hear what they looked like when they were born, the function of the umbilical cord, the role of the doctor in the delivery, and other details.

A discussion of birth should also include information about cesarean deliveries:

Parent: "Sometimes it isn't possible for the baby to be born through the woman's vagina. Maybe the baby isn't facing the right way, or the mother is too small. When that happens, the doctor makes a small cut in the woman's abdomen and in her uterus and takes the baby out that way."

Child: "Does the doctor ever cut the baby?"

Parent: "No, the doctor is very careful and doesn't cut the baby."

Child: "Does it hurt when he cuts the mother?"

Parent: "The mother receives some special medicine so that she doesn't feel the cut."

Remember to add whatever details about the child's birth that will make it seem special, such as who attended the birth, what people said when she was born, what she looked like, whether she cried or not, and where she was born.

Around the age of seven or eight, children who have been adopted often think they were placed for adoption because they were somehow defective. Make sure to add something to the birth story that indicates how satisfactory the baby was at birth, especially if there is anything, such as the baby needing immediate medical attention, crying loudly, or being "all red and wrinkled," that a child might think would be unacceptable to a parent, and therefore a reason to "give the child away."

If you don't know the details of your child's birth and have no way of finding them out, you can explain what probably happened. Whenever you do this, be sure you label the discussion as "probable" rather than as fact.

Parent: "We don't know where you were born, but in the
country you were born in, women often have their
babies at home, so you probably weren't born in a
hospital, but in your mother's house."

Biologic and adopted children

Parents who have both adopted and biologic children have
told me they worry that if they talk about the pregnancy and
birth of the biologic child, the adopted child will feel uncomfortable or slighted. But each of your children needs to hear
the story of how she was born and joined your family. You
should not try to compensate for not giving birth to one of
your children by ignoring the birth stories of the other
children in the family. Consider that the child who is adopted
may tell her sibling, "Mom and dad chose me; they had to take
you." If your biologic child hasn't heard you talk enthusias-
tically about when you were pregnant with her, she may be
vulnerable to such taunts. Tell the story of your pregnancy
and the child's birth with sincere joy and enthusiasm. And
don't feel this has to be done outside the hearing of the child
who is adopted. One mother told me that she was surprised to
find her adopted children fascinated by the story of her
biologic child's gestation and birth. She realized it was their
only chance to hear about conception, pregnancy, and birth in
a personal way.

Growing understanding of adoption

Usually a general discussion of reproduction and birth
will lead to the question, "Did I grow in your uterus,
mommy?" Adoptive parents often swallow hard when they
hear this question, recognizing that an honest answer will
lead the child to an understanding that she is adopted. But
because they have waited and prepared for this question,
parents may misunderstand what the child really wants to
know. Chances are the young child is not asking whether or

not she was adopted, but whether or not she grew inside her mother like other babies. Since you are the only mother she knows (even though she may have been told about other mothers), naturally she asks, "Did I grow in *your* uterus, mommy?" If you answer only the adoption part of that question, the child may end up confused. The response, "No, you didn't grow inside me. Mommy and daddy couldn't make a baby that would grow inside mommy. We got you from an adoption agency," implies that the child didn't grow inside her mother like other children – a common misconception for children who are adopted. Even though your child may not be asking if she was adopted when she asks if she grew in your uterus, use the opportunity to explain that she was adopted, while also addressing the child's more immediate question:

Child: "Did I grow in your uterus, mommy?"

Parent: "You grew inside a woman, just like all babies do, but not inside me. And you came out of her just like other babies do. But the other woman wasn't able to take care of a baby, so after you were born, you came to live with us and became our baby."

In the story you tell your child about her adoption, the sequence of events shouldn't imply that the child was responsible for what happened. For example, if the child's birthmother died as a result of complications due to the birth, separate discussions of the child's birth from discussions of the birthmother's death so that the child isn't left feeling responsible:

". . . You grew inside your birthmother just like all babies do, and when it was time for you to be born, you came out of your birthmother just like all babies do. Your birthmother told your father how beautiful she thought you were and they were very happy."

Later the parent can add: "When you were one day old,

your father got a call from the doctor who told him
your birthmother had a serious infection. This
sometimes happens to people, and usually the doctor
can give the person medicine to stop the infection. But
the medicine didn't work for your birthmother and she
died."

While you may have told your child the story of her adoption many times before, and she may have repeated it with
such skill that you were sure she understood what she was
saying, she was probably just repeating what she had been
told. Not until she understands reproduction will she have a
real understanding of what it means to be adopted. Then,
hearing of her adoption may be like hearing the story for the
first time. She may ask questions you've answered before or
may not seem to know details she's been told before.

Particularly with a four- or five-year-old, some questions
may be less intended to gain information than to enjoy the
asking. If this seems to be the case, try asking the child her
opinion of the question. That may be just what she wants you
to do, and you may gain some special insight into how she is
thinking and feeling.

In talking about birth and adoption, don't be misled by a
young child's seemingly sophisticated vocabulary. Children
four, five, and six years old enjoy using new words and may
even use difficult words appropriately without fully com-
prehending their meaning. This can fool parents into thinking
the child understands what she is saying long before she has
the intellectual capability to do so. Continue to speak in concrete rather than abstract terms and continue to explain complex ideas in simple, understandable ways. In other words,
tell your preschooler the story of her adoption in much the
same way you told it to her when she was a toddler.

Children develop at different rates, and developmental
stages overlap birthdays. Some preschoolers will continue to
confuse the various ways children join families, while others

will clearly differentiate between them.

It's often around the age of six that the child develops a much clearer idea of the different ways children join families. Six is a transition age in which the child is getting ready to leave the home-centered world for the school-centered world. She's becoming more social and more independent. At the same time, the prospect of leaving her familiar world can cause the six-year-old to regress. Her new understanding of concepts such as language, time, and space enable her to understand conception, birth, and alternative forms of parenthood in ways that the younger child may not. Her developing mental skills – to reason, learn rules, and perform trial and error mentally – indicate her readiness for school, and will lead eventually to new levels of understanding – and concern – about the way in which she joined her family, which are discussed in Chapters 4 and 5.

Feelings about adoption

Children four, five, and six generally accept being adopted. They accept their family even if by societal standards it is nontraditional. They don't understand yet that most children live with their biologic mother and father, but even if they did, they would be unlikely to care that their family is different. They live in the here and now – accepting what is within their experience because they can't imagine that life could be different. They can't yet imagine something as true if it is contrary to their belief or opinion. (This is part of the reason why the child this age may ask over and over again, "Can we go to the park?" even though she has been repeatedly told, "Not today.") Knowing they are adopted is unlikely to result in children this age feeling rejected, strange, or defective. Nevertheless, they may ask questions or express feelings that surprise you.

Allow your child an opportunity to express her feelings and be honest about your own feelings. One mother told me how a touching discussion of adoption developed when her son watched a friend nurse her newborn baby:

Child: "How did you feed me when I was a baby – from a bottle?"

Parent: "Yes. I wanted to breastfeed you, but it isn't easy to breastfeed a baby unless you give birth to him."

Child: "You're sad about that, aren't you?"

Parent: "Yes, I'm sad. I wish I could have given birth to you and nursed you."

By sharing her feelings, this mother and her child experienced a profound sense of closeness, and the child learned it's all right to express his feelings about being adopted, even if they aren't always happy ones.

Tuning in to adoption messages

Discussions of reproduction and adoption may end with a cuddle or feeling of closeness, but with a young child, they just as often end with the child springing off the mother's lap in search of diversion. Parents are left wondering if they were unclear or said too much. Just because the child didn't express much of a reaction doesn't mean that she didn't have one or won't have one in the future as she internalizes the remarkable information she's been given.

Because children this age express themselves through their play, you may get clues to how your child has interpreted information by paying attention when she is playing with her friends. Unlike toddlers who want to play primarily with things, preschool children are shifting their interest to other children. And the same mental development that has expanded their language, that is, the ability to understand symbols, allows them to engage in fantasy play. By putting on a bonnet the preschooler "becomes" a baby; a sword fashioned of construction paper enables her to "become" a hero.

Big and little; good and bad

Most preschoolers will play house or doctor, or re-enact their favorite characters from Saturday morning cartoons. Usually, their play involves two main themes: big vs. little, and bad vs. good. The child this age is often told she is either too little to do something (cross the street), or too big to do something (suck her thumb). By discovering that she can be both big and little at the same time—both the baby and the parent—she learns how to "parent" herself, which we know as self-control. She learns this by sometimes playing the baby and sometimes the grown-up. As pediatrician Vera Fahlberg points out, you will hardly ever see a four-year-old playing a four-year-old.

Children this age also need to learn that they can be both bad and good at the same time so they grow up knowing that it's okay to make mistakes. If this developmental step is missed, children may feel that if they can't be good all the time (and who can?), they must be bad all the time. Again, they learn to integrate these aspects of human nature by sometimes playing the hero and sometimes the evil character.

You may observe that your child sometimes plays the "bad baby." Most children will, so that is not something to be concerned about. Nevertheless, because children often think they were adopted because they were "bad from birth," you might want to reinforce the idea that your child's behavior had nothing to do with her being placed for adoption, especially if your child seems to play the "bad baby" exclusively:

Parent: "What were you and Beth playing?"

Child: "House."

Parent: "Who were you?"

Child: "I was the baby. Beth was the mommy."

Parent: "What did you do as a baby?"

Child: "I was a bad baby. I cried all the time."

Parent: "Do you think a baby is bad if he cries?"

Child: "Uh-huh."

Parent: "Do you think you ever cried when you were a baby?"

Child: "I don't know. Did I?"

Parent: "Sure. Crying is the way babies tell their parents that they need something because they don't know any words. When a baby cries, her parents know that she needs to be fed, or doesn't feel well, or needs her diaper changed. Parents don't think a baby is bad because she cries."

Child: "When I cried did you feed me?"

Parent: "If you were hungry I did. Sometimes you cried because you were tired. Then I put you to bed. And sometimes I didn't know why you were crying and nothing I could do made you stop. That was very frustrating for me because I wanted you to feel good. And I bet it was frustrating for you not to be able to tell me exactly what you needed. But even though I was frustrated, I still loved you."

Depending on how the conversation is going, you might want to explore the topic further:

Parent: "Do you think that babies are ever bad in other ways besides crying?"

Child: "Sometimes they wet their diaper."

Parent: "Is that bad?"

Child: "Well, they can't help it."

Parent: "That's right. So it's okay. Perhaps there are times when you wet the bed or wet your pants even though you aren't a baby. That doesn't make you bad, either."

Magical thinking

Parents can also get clues to how well their child understands reproduction and adoption (as well as other important subjects) by listening for signs of "magical think-ing" by their child. Preschoolers believe that if one event hap-pens after another event, the first event caused the second to happen. For this reason, and because children this age are still quite self-centered, if they wish for something to happen and it happens, they believe it happened because they wished for it. This can have serious consequences for a child who tells her sibling, "I hope you choke," only to have the sibling choke. The child then feels all-powerful and guilty for using her power to cause harm to her sibling. It's easy to see, then, that if a parent says to a preschooler, "Would you like to have a lit-tle brother?" and the child responds, "Yes," and the next day the parents come home from the adoption agency with a little brother, that the child may believe she is responsible. And in her mind, if she could make the little brother arrive, a simple wish or request could make the little brother leave.

Vera Fahlberg suggests that parents pay attention to anything their child says that just doesn't seem to make sense because it can provide clues to magical thinking that the child is using to explain an event. For example:

Child: "If grandma dies, will we get a new puppy?"
Parent: "No, why do you think we would get a new puppy if grandma dies?"
Child: "When our cat died we got a new puppy."

Racial awareness and attitudes

One mother was concerned to see her four-year-old Asian–American son pulling at the corners of his eyes in an effort to "look Chinese." She wondered if she should point out to "Kirk" that his eyes were already almond-shaped. She wondered if he was confused about his racial heritage because he was being raised by Euro–American parents. She wondered if she should point out that it isn't kind to make fun of people because of their physical characteristics. Not knowing what to do, she ignored his actions, and that was probably the best reaction.

During the preschool years, children become increasingly aware of the differences between people. By the age of four, children understand that people belong to different groups distinguished from other groups by physical features. By the age of five, they have had enough experiences of their own, and have perceived enough verbal and nonverbal messages to understand that different racial groups have different social status. By the age of six, they know to what racial group they belong.

This understanding of race develops gradually in children as a result of their increasing ability to notice differences, understand which attributes people can change and which they can't, and classify people according to common characteristics. Racial attitudes develop as a result of children's experiences and the attitudes they perceive in those around them. Attempts to teach children about race before they have the mental ability to notice differences and classify items are therefore a waste of time, and may even be counterproductive.

The first racial characteristic that children are aware of is skin color. Experts believe infants are aware of skin color differences. Recognition of eye shape, hair texture, and other "secondary" racial characteristics comes later, although we do not know exactly when. So the fact that Kirk recognized that Chinese people have almond-shaped eyes but wasn't aware of his own almond-shaped eyes is not surprising.

The child who remarks on differences in skin color or other racial characteristics is not expressing prejudice. It is a normal part of child development to notice differences. In fact, the child who does not point out such differences probably has picked up the message somewhere that it's not okay to talk about such differences, and may conclude that differences are "bad." If Kirk's mother had told him it wasn't kind to pretend to look Chinese, he probably would have been confused; he was just trying to experience what it would be like to be Chinese.

Parents should respond to children's comments about racial characteristics matter-of-factly, reinforcing correct ideas and providing information to correct misconceptions:

Child: "If Jennifer touches me, will my skin get dirty, too?"

Parent: "Jennifer's skin isn't dirty. It's dark. She was born with dark skin because her mother and father had dark skin. Her skin will always be dark, just like your skin will always be light. But inside, Jennifer and you and all people are the same."

Child: "If I play in the mud my skin will be dark."

Parent: "Your skin will still be light. But we won't be able to see it because of the brown mud on top of it."

Racial confusion

One of the problems preschool children have in understanding racial differences is related to their difficulty believing one person can be two things at once. They believe that if a group is alike in one way, it must be alike in all ways, so they have difficulty understanding that someone can be both male and East Indian-American. A child may say, "Peter has dark skin because he is a boy" even though she knows other boys who have light skin. Don't worry about these kinds of comments. People do not grow up believing that someone's race is determined by her gender. This kind of confusion works itself out as the child develops the mental ability to understand that people can be both alike and different. Matter-of-factly correct your child's misconception, but don't be concerned if she doesn't grasp what you're saying immediately:

Child: "Daddy's Korean, too."

Parent: "Why do you think daddy's Korean?"

Child: "He has black hair, and I have black hair."

Parent: "You have black hair because your birthparents had black hair. Most people in Korea have black hair. But people in other parts of the world have black hair, too. Daddy has black hair, but he isn't Korean."

This might be an opportunity to explore your child's feelings about being Korean in a Euro-American family:

Parent: "Do you sometimes wish daddy were Korean?"

Child: "Yes."

Parent: "Why would you like that?"

Child: "Then I wouldn't be the only one who was different."

Children's awareness of their own race

Four-year-olds, such as Kirk, generally do not know to which race they belong, although they may sometimes repeat what they have heard others say. Children are able to identify themselves by race as a result of the cues they get from people around them, but also as a result of mental development that enables them to group people or objects according to common characteristics, which usually develops around the age of six. (This new ability to classify objects leads the child this age to develop an interest in "collections," such as baseball cards, shells, and butterflies.) While parents can refer to a child's racial group when it is appropriate to do so, trying to "teach" a child racial self-classification before the child has the necessary mental development may result in the child feeling anxious or lead to racial bias.

One parent noticed that an elderly relative frequently made unnecessary comments about his child's ethnic group, such as, "My eye doctor is from India." While the comments were positive statements, they made the parent feel uncomfortable, and he thought his child must be uncomfortable, too. The parent in a situation like that can gently take the relative aside and say something like:

> "Aunt Harriet, I appreciate your interest in Sam and in India. I know you intend for your comments about India to make Sam feel accepted, but I think it might be making Sam feel different."

If your child's birthparents are of different races, social worker Azizi Powell says that telling the child she is "biracial" or of "mixed race" does her a disservice. Most people identify a person by one race rather than a mixture. A child who appears to be African–American will be treated as African–American even though she may have one Euro–American parent. A child with no African heritage at all will be treated as an African–American if her skin is very dark. A child with little skin color may be treated as Euro–American even if she is descended from African–American people.

While we might hope that a child of one Euro–American and one African–American would be treated as an equal member of both races, our society will classify them, and treat them, on the basis of their appearance.

Parents will therefore want to expose their children to all the cultures of their heritage and be honest about the races of their birthparents, but not try to convince their children that they are a different race than they appear to be. It simply won't make sense to the child, and it won't help the child to think of herself as "biracial" if everyone else considers her to be African–American. Nor is it necessary to "correct" someone who makes incorrect assumptions about the child's race as a result of the child's appearance.

More than one parent has expressed concern to me about allowing their child of mixed racial heritage to "pass" as a Euro–American. Parents are not denying her heritage by allowing her and others to think of her as Euro–American as long as they are incorporating aspects of her total cultural heritage into their family life – and as long as their assessment of her physical appearance is accurate and not "wishful thinking."

Awareness of nationality

Preschool children have a concept of faraway places. They may have grandparents or other relatives who live in other cities or states. They may have friends in their preschool from other countries. They can understand that they were born in a different place far away, but "far away" to them means anywhere that isn't right here. The concept of political and geographical boundaries is too abstract for them to understand. While using a map or globe to explain where they were born may seem helpful, it presumes that the child can understand how the world can be represented cartographically, and that is not likely for the vast majority of preschoolers. Because preschoolers can understand symbols, they can understand that a certain flag represents Colombia or that a particular combination of colors on an Olympic athlete means he's from Korea, but they won't understand that Colombia and Korea are countries with particular governments. They are just places. However, preschoolers can understand that different people have different physical features, wear different clothing, speak different languages, and have different customs. So in trying to help your child understand her nationality, concentrate on these aspects of her culture rather than geography.

Child: "Aaron said I'm from Mexico. Am I from Mexico?"

Parent: "No, you were born in a country called El Salvador. Aaron may have thought you were from Mexico because people in Mexico look very much like people from El Salvador. But Mexico is a different place from El Salvador. Would you like to play a game that children in El Salvador play?"

In a few years, when your child is able to understand the idea of citizenship and countries, talks like these will have given her a sound basis for understanding that she came from another country and will let her know that she can talk about that country and be proud of her origins.

Establishing ties with extended family

The sense of being connected to previous generations is not something that can be taken for granted in a family not genetically related. The preschool years are a good time to encourage contact between children and their extended family so adoptees feel membership in their family extends beyond their parents and siblings.

Children who are not raised by their biologic parents sometimes grow up feeling somewhat cut off from their extended family. They grow up knowing that they joined their family because their parents wanted very much to have them. And they believe, because they have experienced it, that you don't have to be biologically related to someone to love them as though you were. They grow up thinking of their adoptive parents as their parents because they raised them and think of their adoptive siblings as their brothers and sisters because they were raised together as brother and sister. But as one adoptee told me, when it comes to relatives outside the immediate family, the sense of "belonging" may not be as strong.

What links generations is common ancestry–a shared history and shared genetic pool. We talk about our "forebears" and "ancestors," and speak of ourselves as "descendants." We speak of family heirlooms passed down from generation to generation so that we have a connection to the past and so the items stay "in the family."

Today's young parents are unlikely to live in the same state as their parents or grandparents, much less the same neighborhood. They have probably exceeded the previous generation in terms of formal education. Having grown up in an era of rapid technological change, their values, eating habits, religious beliefs, and overall lifestyle are likely to be far different from their parents' and grandparents'. For many adults, the only connection they feel to their extended family is a shared ethnic heritage.

It isn't surprising, then, that someone who has never lived with these relatives and who doesn't share their historical, genetic, or ethnic heritage may feel cut off. And, indeed, many adults who were adopted, such as those quoted in John Triseliotis' book *In Search of Origins* (Boston: Routledge & Kegan Paul, 1973), tell us that while they felt like a member of their immediate family, they never felt like a valid member of their "tribe" or "clan."

Naturally, not all people who have been adopted feel this way. But neither can it be assumed that children will feel connected to their extended families. Parents who want their children to feel accepted and loved by their extended family must give their children and relatives opportunities to develop relationships based on shared experiences.

Relationships with the extended biologic family

Parents who have an open adoption may find that while the birthmother typically wants a lot of contact with her child during the first year after placement, her need for contact often diminishes after that first year. She has been reassured that her child is being well cared for, has seen the child through the "first tooth," "first Christmas," and "first birthday," and needs to proceed with her life, which was interrupted by the pregnancy.

For this reason, adoptive families often find that the most consistent contact they have with their child's biologic family during the preschool years is with the biologic grandparents, especially if the child is the first grandchild.

Parents who adopt an older child may find that while the birthparents had problems that prevented their providing the child with consistent nurturing, the biologic grandparents have been important people in the child's life.

Take advantage of contact with extended biologic family members if it is available. It is important for your child to feel a connection with her extended biologic family. Once again, for the preschooler, the exact relationship may be confusing, but that will become clearer as the child grows. All that is important at this time is that the child knows these are "special people" in her life.

Activity: Getting to know the extended family

While geographical distance, different values, and less dependence on the extended family typical of today's families makes interaction more difficult, with a little effort and commitment, quality relationships can be established – even long-distance.

The earlier your child has contact with her relatives, the more likely the relatives will be to accept the child into the family. In fact, it is best to involve them even before the child arrives. The preschool years offer some good opportunities for enhancing the relationship that may have begun in infancy.

Preschoolers, while they may not quite understand relationships well enough to know why someone is their grandmother or aunt, have no difficulty understanding that these are special people. They enjoy talking on the telephone, getting mail, and visiting. Unlike some older children who may find a visit with relatives boring or a telephone call more obligation than entertainment, preschoolers are enthusiastic about having contact with their extended family.

Parents who have used this natural enthusiasm to enhance the relationship between their child and the child's extended family have offered these suggestions:

• Allow your child to talk on the telephone when you're

talking to relatives. Allow them to call when they have special news to share, not just on birthdays and holidays.

• Encourage correspondence between your child and your relatives. While your child may not be old enough to write, she can dictate a letter or story to you or into a tape recorder. (Such activities are important pre-reading skills.) It's important to write down what your child says even though it may seem stream-of-conscious, silly, or even a bit impolite. The letter that says: "Thank you for the dress you sent me for my birthday. I wanted a football," may not please the etiquette experts, but it goes a long way toward helping the relative get to know your child because it is her sincere expression, not something made up for the occasion. And it will be a far more treasured letter to the relative than one that expresses the "correct" sentiment, but was obviously composed by the parent.

Sometimes relatives feel awkward about writing to children because they don't know what to say, but they are open to ideas. Some parents suggest that they enclose a sticker, baseball card, or balloon in a card, or that they clip a magazine article or picture from the newspaper that the child might like to see or have read to her. A relative known for his sense of humor could send a riddle. Picture post cards are also important ways of communicating.

• Buy your relatives a tape recorder (if they don't already have one) and encourage them to exchange tapes with your child. Children love to hear themselves tape recorded. If they aren't verbal enough to spontaneously fill up a thirty-minute tape, you can conduct an "interview" with them about your latest camping trip or the cat that took up residence on your doorstep. At the very least you can take an idea from Sesame Street and interview them about what happened when the Three Little Pigs built their house. Suggest that your relatives record stories about the important events in their lives or in the family history. Children this age particularly like to hear stories about things their parents did when they were children. One of the most precious possessions of my children is a tape their great-grandmother made for them reading children's stories from books checked out of the library.

• When your children have contact with their relatives, try to encourage them to do a particular activity. It is sometimes hard for a child to remember something about a relative she only sees occasionally, but it is much easier if they can think of the person as "the uncle that does the card tricks," "the aunt that takes you fishing," or "the grandma with all the cats." With a little thought, even a trip to visit a relative in a nursing home – sometimes depressing or scary to young children – can be a pleasant memory. On one memorable visit, my daughter taught her great-grandmother to play the card game Crazy 8's. Take some vegetable seeds or bedding plants along for your child to plant with her grandfather; bring a box of ready-to-mix cookies for your child to bake with her great-aunt, and help the relatives to see, if they don't seem to, that what is important is the memories that are being created, not the plants or the cookies.

• Each family has its own traditions when it comes to gifts. Some grandparents have difficulty shopping or don't see their grandchildren often enough to know what they would like to have. They feel more comfortable giving money. Others enjoy sending expensive presents or taking their grandchildren on shopping excursions. If it appears your relatives need and will accept some gift-giving advice, you can make suggestions for gifts that will enhance your child's relationship with that relative. For example, children this age love to receive mail, and there are many magazines published for them. While they might give little attention to the card under the Christmas tree that says their grandparents are sending them a subscription to a magazine, that magazine will keep arriving long after most of the other presents under the Christmas tree are forgotten or broken. It's your job as parents to remind the child each month, "Grandma sent you another magazine." If there is a craft or activity in the magazine, suggest that your child do it and send the finished product to grandma. Most children this age need an endless supply of art materials, which can be easily purchased at any discount store. Be sure your child then sends a special picture to the relative who supplied the construction paper and markers.

When it's time to reciprocate, allow your child to make the selection. You can direct your child a little bit, but allow her to make the final choice. For example, suggest that she send grandma a new coffee mug and take her to a store with a good assortment, but let her select the one she wants. Ask her why she picked the one she did, and enclose a card giving her an explanation. Children this age have remarkable memories and enjoy participating in a tradition. Each year my daughter picks out a charm to send to her godmother. We try to select something that indicates something important she did that year or an interest she has developed. You could also establish a tradition of giving a kitchen towel each year or a piece of fishing tackle. Calendars with attractive, glossy photographs are usually welcome and useful items. Each year a child could pick out a new calendar, with her choice either reflecting her interests or those of the recipient.

• One of the gifts my daughter received when she was quite small was quite a treasure. My sister and her son made my daughter a story book introducing her extended family. It began, "You not only have a mommy and daddy who love you very much, but a lot of other relatives, too." Each page of the book features one relative. There is a colored pencil drawing of the relative, a small photograph, and a description of the relationship of the person to my child. For example: "This is your Uncle Dan. He is married to your Aunt Jo. Aunt Jo is your mommy's sister." Each page also contains a description of the person featured, such as a job or favorite activity. As my daughter's extended family has grown with marriages and the births of new cousins, we've added to this story book. A family book such as this can help children in nontraditional families sort out their sometimes confusing family relationships. (Suggestions for making a family tree are given at the end of Chapter 5.)

4. "Why Didn't They Keep Me?"
The Middle Childhood Years

The school years are a time of information gathering and problem solving, and those activities are not confined to the classroom. The mental development that makes it possible for children to begin formal education around the age of seven – to think without using words, to categorize and see relationships, and to test ideas using trial and error – enables children to examine adoption in ways that they were previously incapable of.

As a result, these middle years – the ages from about seven to eleven – are critical years for children who have been adopted, but the importance of this time is sometimes overlooked by parents and even professionals.

I've found that a chief complaint of many adoptive parent groups is that their members become inactive when their children reach school age. Adoption issues seem to be less important, and other activities, such as Scouts and athletics, compete for the time and energy families have available.

Furthermore, the middle years of childhood tend to be calm, quiet, "easy" years compared to the demanding preschool years and the confrontational adolescent years. But a lot of thinking about adoption is going on in the minds of children seven to eleven years old, and some of these thoughts are disturbing.

When children enter school, they become aware of how much is going on in the world outside of their experience. They also are exposed to more diversity. They find people have different physical and mental abilities, different lifestyles, different beliefs, and different appearances. Most importantly, they realize that most people are not adopted, and they want to know why they are not like other people and what they have lost by being adopted.

This leads children to wonder why they were placed for adoption and what their birthparents are like. It also leads to feelings of sadness and anger as they grieve for what might have been. Talking with children about these issues is the focus of this chapter.

But there are other issues during the middle childhood years. Children are also concerned with their place in their family and their place in their social world. Their feelings about their adoptive families, the attitudes of other people toward adoption, and their racial status can contribute in significant ways to their self-image. These topics will be explored in Chapter 5.

Limits to children's understanding

As children in middle childhood try to apply their new problem-solving capability to adoption questions, they are hampered by their immature reasoning abilities and their lack of sophistication about the world.

When children this age try to test a hypothesis and the facts lead to a conclusion other than the one they expected, they are more likely to try to change the facts to fit the conclusion than to change the conclusion to fit the facts. For example, if a child says, "When I grow up I'm going to fly in a spaceship to another galaxy," he might be confronted with facts that demonstrate that such an adventure would take more than a lifetime. Rather than accept the seemingly logical conclusion, the child might say, "First I'll invent a spaceship that would go faster than the speed of light."

Children therefore tend to oversimplify problems, apply simple solutions, and become frustrated when their view of the situation is inconsistent with reality.

Dealing with complicated issues like adoption are at best distracting, and sometimes disturbing, for children in the middle years. They need a concrete way of looking at adoption issues and a great deal of support as they sort out information and react emotionally to what they learn.

Understanding the birthmother

Children in the middle years wonder why things happen, and a primary concern for those who have been adopted is why their birthmothers didn't keep them. Eventually they will also have questions about their birthfathers, but their initial interest is in their birthmothers.

While you may not want to tell your child everything you know about the birthmother's situation until your child is mature enough to understand it, you can make sure you don't mislead your child or knowingly say something that will be contradicted by the truth.

Traditional adoption

In the case of a traditional adoption, the child's reasoning might go something like this:

Child: "Why didn't my birthmother keep me?"

Parent: "She was very young. She was only seventeen. She wasn't married. She hadn't finished high school yet, so she didn't have a good job to get the money necessary to take care of a baby. But most importantly, people are physically able to make a baby long before they know how to take care of a baby. She wasn't ready to be the parent of any baby. She didn't think she'd

know the best ways to take care of a baby. She wanted
you to be with a family who could take good care of
you."

Child: "Why didn't she ask her parents to help her take
care of me?"

Parent: "I don't know. Maybe she thought it would be too
hard to have a baby at home even with a lot of help.
What if you wanted to watch television, and she
thought you had watched enough television, but her
mother said it was okay for you to watch television?
They might argue about it, and you might be confused
about who makes the rules."

Child: "I'd listen to my mother because too much television isn't good for you."

Parent: "That might be the right choice in that situation,
but because your mother was so young, in a lot of situations she might make the wrong decision."

Child: "Then I'd do what my grandmother said."

It's clear that the child here is determined to manipulate
the situation to show that his birthmother could have kept
him because that's what he wants to believe. While he is in
this frame of mind, it's doubtful any explanation will shake his
conviction that his birthmother could have kept him. As we'll
discuss later in this chapter, the child's limited ability to
understand the birthparent's decision and accept evidence
contrary to what the child wants to believe may lead him to
some troubling conclusions.

Single mothers

Child: "A kid in my class was born when his mother was
only nineteen and she wasn't married."

Because so few women with an unplanned pregnancy
choose an adoption plan today, your child is going to encounter children at school whose mothers were in the same

situation as your child's, but who chose to keep their children. Women don't choose adoption because they are young or because they are unmarried, or even because they are poor. They choose adoption because *they feel unprepared to raise a child*. Often poverty, lack of education, youth, and marital status contribute to their being unable to raise a child, but it is the birthmother's awareness of her inability to be a parent that is the critical factor.

You can point out to your child that you don't have to be a certain age or be married or have a certain kind of job to be a good parent. But you do need maturity, experience, and stability. Ask your child to describe the kinds of qualities a good parent needs. One parent was surprised at his child's insight.

Parent: "What do you think you need to be a good parent?"

Child: "You should love your child."

Parent: "Yes, what else?"

Child: "You should have enough money."

Parent: "Do you think if you love your child and have enough money to buy him clothes and food, that makes you a good parent?"

Child: "No, you need to be patient, and teach him the right things to do."

Parent: "That's right. A lot of mothers love their babies very much, and sometimes they even have enough money to take care of them, but mothers and fathers are responsible for helping their children grow up. That takes food and a healthy place to live. But it also means, as you point out, learning how to make choices so that when you become an adult you can take care of yourself. If you aren't grown up yourself, it's hard to help someone else grow up."

Child: "You might not know the right things to do yourself, so you couldn't tell your child the right things to do."

Parent: "That's right. The problem is that most people's bodies are grown up enough when they are thirteen to make babies. But most thirteen-year-olds are not grown up enough in other ways to be able to raise a child to make good choices. Some people are grown up enough when they are nineteen to raise children, but some people aren't grown up enough even when they're thirty. When you were five years old, you could ride a two-wheeler, and you wanted very much to ride your bike in the street. You promised us that you would be careful, but you weren't mature enough to make the right choices and you might have gotten hurt. So even though you could ride your bike in the street and you wanted to make the right decisions, you had to wait until mommy and daddy were sure you would be able to make the right choices."

The "mature" birthmother

Sometimes the standard explanation, "Your birthmother couldn't take care of any baby," seems to fly in the face of the facts. Some children are placed for adoption by married women, women with other children, women in stable relationships, women in their twenties or thirties, women with good jobs. In these situations it is probably more accurate to say, "She couldn't take care of any baby born to her at this time in her life." The more you know about her situation, of course, the easier it will be to explain why that was the case. Perhaps she realized that without a job or a high school diploma, caring for one baby is hard enough and knew that she wouldn't be able to take care of a second. Perhaps she was having personal problems that she believed would distract her from the needs of an infant. (See "Explaining difficult situations" later in this chapter.) Whatever the circumstances, emphasize that it was her circumstances and not some quality in the child or lack of concern for the child that resulted in the adoption plan. Placing a baby for adoption is done by a woman who *at this point in her life* feels unable to care for a child.

Child: "Why didn't my birthmother keep me?"

Parent: "She decided she couldn't take care of a baby born to her at the time you were born."

Child: "Why not?"

Parent: "Your birthmother already had two children. When she had those children she was married and had a husband who could help her with a family by getting a job and by helping to care for the children. When you were born she didn't have a husband. She was trying to figure out how she could get a job and take care of those children, and she knew it would be even harder with a new baby because all babies take a lot of care. So she decided to place you for adoption because she knew that your adoptive parents would be able to take care of a baby."

Child: "Did she place her other kids for adoption?"

Parent: "No, she didn't."

Child: "Why not?"

Parent: "They had lived together for several years and her children were used to having her for a mother. She probably thought that it would be difficult for her other children to get used to a new mother, but if she placed the new baby with other parents, they could get used to each other from the beginning."

Intercountry adoptions

This is how you might explain the situation for birth-mothers in Korea:

Parent: "In Korea, it's very embarrassing for a woman who isn't married to have a child. It embarrasses her and it embarrasses her family. And in Korea, like in other parts of Asia, children are brought up to never embarrass their families. So even though your birth-mother might have decided that she didn't care what people thought of her having a child and not a husband, she wouldn't want to embarrass her family."

Child: "Why didn't she just take me and move away?"

Parent: "In Korea, if your mother isn't married to your father, it would also be very embarrassing for you. You wouldn't be able to go to school or get a job when you got older."

Child: "Why not?"

Parent: "It's a little bit like pretending you don't even exist because your mother wasn't married to your father."

Child: "That's stupid."

Parent: "It's different from the way things are in this country, but it's the way things are in Korea. And your birthmother probably knew that if she placed you for adoption that you would come to the United States where you would have a chance to go to school and have a job when you got older."

Birthmothers through surrogacy

The answer to the question "Why didn't my mother keep me?" is a little different when the child was adopted as a result of an intentional pregnancy by a surrogate mother. Most birthmothers who become involved with surrogacy are able to take care of a baby; in fact, most have biologic children. So while the emphasis in a traditional adoption is on the birthmother's inability to care for any baby, the emphasis in a surrogate adoption is on the birthmother's motives for getting pregnant. Many of these birthmothers have friends or family members who have experienced infertility or adoption. They also become involved with surrogacy because they like being pregnant but don't want any more children. Parents who have an opportunity to meet their child's birthmother can learn details about her motives that can be helpful in explaining them to their child:

Parent: "Your birthmother had three children whom she loved very much. She was sad when she heard mommy couldn't grow a baby inside her. She wanted to help us have a baby so that we could be as happy as she was."

Child: "Didn't she want to keep me?"

Parent: "She got pregnant with you because she wanted mommy and daddy to have a baby. She always thought of you as our baby that she was helping us have."

Child: "Why would she want to have a baby for somebody else?"

Parent: "Your birthmother knew what it was like to want a baby very much and not be able to have one because her sister and brother-in-law couldn't make a baby. Your birthmother liked being pregnant and thought it was something she did well. She didn't want any more children for herself, but she thought that by having a baby for us she could help us by doing something she liked to do. Is there anything you share with people because you like to do it and can do it very well?"

Child: "I like to draw pictures for people."

Parent: "Do you remember the time Grandma asked you to draw some flowers for her?"

Child: "I worked real hard on it and it turned out really well."

Parent: "I remember that you liked it so much you sort of wanted to keep it. But you gave it to Grandma because all the time you were making it, you were making it for her."

Child: "She really liked it."

Parent: "I think that's kind of how your birthmother felt. If something had happened to daddy and mommy so that we couldn't raise you, I'm sure she would have taken care of you herself. But even though it was probably hard for her, she placed you with us for adoption because that's why she got pregnant."

Child: "What if she had decided she wanted to keep me?"

Parent: "We can imagine what would have happened then, but that isn't what happened. She decided to keep her promise, and we're glad she did because we love you very much."

Birthmothers of children adopted through surrogacy have told me they would explain their motives to their children by pointing out that had it not been for the agreement between them and the adoptive parents, the children would not exist— they were intentionally conceived for the adoptive parents. But just as children placed for adoption as a result of an unintentional pregnancy should not have to feel grateful to their adoptive parents for "rescuing" them, children adopted through surrogacy should not have to feel grateful to their parents for creating them. The birthmothers involved in surrogacy have needs that are met through the adoption—to help other people by doing something that they think they're good at. That is not to say that placing a baby for adoption through surrogacy doesn't involve some sadness, but neither is it entirely selfless.

The explanation for a surrogate gestational mother (a woman who agrees to carry a child unrelated to her) would be similar to that of a birthmother through surrogacy.

Biologic mothers through in vitro fertilization

Donating an egg is physically more complicated than donating sperm because it requires a surgical procedure. Implanting a fertilized egg in the uterus of a woman is a fairly recent development compared to donor insemination. Consequently, there are far fewer children conceived as a result of a donor egg or donor embryo than by donor insemination. But as medical science and technology advance, *in vitro* fertilization will become more common.

Presumably, just as children adopted by donor insemination have questions and concerns about their birthfathers, children conceived by *in vitro* fertilization will want to know more about their biologic mothers and their motivations.

Parents can explain that like birthmothers involved in

surrogacy, women who donate an egg for *in vitro* fertilization often do so because they understand the difficulty people have conceiving or adopting a child, and want to help. Parents can also say the biologic parents may wonder whether the egg developed into a child and what that child was like.

Stepparent adoptions

Because of child custody practices and the numbers of single women who become pregnant, it is more common today for a child to be adopted by a stepfather than a stepmother. For this reason, a child adopted by a stepmother may need more help understanding why his situation was different:

Parent: "Mommy and daddy decided not to live together any more because we couldn't agree on some very important things. Because mommy was moving to a new city and trying to get a new job, she thought it would be too hard for her to have a child with her, so we decided that you would live with daddy. When daddy married Susan, she became a mother to you. She took care of you when you were sick, helped daddy cook for you, and gradually she learned to love you, and you learned to love her. But she was afraid that if anything happened to daddy, she wouldn't be able to keep being your mother. She wanted to adopt you so she could always be your mother. But she needed your birth-mother's permission to do that, so we sent a letter to your birthmother asking her if it would be okay if Susan adopted you. Your birthmother said it would be okay. It probably made her sad, but she probably realized that since she hadn't seen you in such a long time, and since Susan had been taking such good care of you, that being adopted by Susan was best for you."

Child: "Why hadn't she seen me in a long time?"

Parent: "When you love somebody very much, it's hard to be away from them. Sometimes, if you don't see them for a very long time, it becomes easier to be away from them. But when you see them again, you are reminded how much it hurts to be away from them. I think your birthmother thought she wouldn't miss you as much if she didn't see you at all."

Misunderstanding the birthmother

Because the child in these middle years oversimplifies his birthmother's problems and tends to ignore evidence that conflicts with his preconceived ideas, none of these explanations will make sense to the child who wants to believe that his birthmother could have kept him. Furthermore, none of these explanations really answer the question of why he was "singled out" to be different. So why he was placed for adoption remains a dilemma for him. Very often he doesn't share this ongoing dilemma with his parents because it appears to him that they're only going to give him the same story that he's heard for years—the one that doesn't make sense to him. He is also at an age when he likes to try to work things out for himself.

What the child tries to do is determine for himself the "real reason" he was placed for adoption. And he often imagines that this "real reason" was something awful—too awful for his parents to share with him.

The child is likely to decide that the real reason his birthmother didn't keep him is because there was something wrong with him—because he was physically defective, a "bad" baby, cried too much, or otherwise was unacceptable. Keep this in mind whenever you are talking about why your child was placed for adoption and make sure you never imply that he was responsible for the decision. Family therapist Claudia Jewett suggests saying, "Your birthmother wasn't able to take care of *any* baby" rather than "Your birthmother wasn't able to take care of *you*." But even if you carefully choose your words, your child may still conclude that he was rejected because he somehow didn't measure up.

It is a rare child who will suddenly announce to his

parents that he thinks he was placed for adoption because he was defective. After all, that thought represents a personal rejection that is difficult for a child to verbalize. But in the course of discussing some aspect of his adoption, the child may give a clue that this is what he's thinking.

Child: "Did I look funny when I was born?"

Parent: "All babies look a little wrinkled, but we thought you looked beautiful."

Child: "I think I was probably ugly or maybe I had something wrong with me."

Parent: "What makes you think that?"

Child: "I just think so."

Parent: "Do you think that your birthmother decided not to keep you because there was something wrong with you?"

Child (crying): "Yes."

It's important for you to allow your child to express his feelings. Responding by saying, "Oh that's just silly," will not make the child feel better, and may keep him from confiding in you the next time. Instead, realize that he sincerely believes something terrible was wrong with him when he was born and that this knowledge is causing him great pain. Then, correct his misunderstanding, offering proof, if possible. One mother whose daughter had difficulty believing there was nothing wrong with her when she was born told the girl that a physician had done a complete examination of her when she was born and offered to call the doctor for a copy of his report. The daughter was delighted to hear of the existence of such a report and encouraged her mother to call for a copy. Evidently, just knowing that there was proof that she was all right was enough. By the time the copy arrived in the mail, the daughter had lost interest in it.

Understanding the birthfather

While children understand how babies are made by about the age of six, their primary interest is in babies and not in how they are made. They are interested in how babies grow, how they are born, and the role of the mother. Somewhere around the age of nine, however, they become more aware of the technical aspects of reproduction and therefore are more interested in the father's role.

Your child needs to know not only the technical role his biologic father played in his life, but also what his birthfather is like, whether the birthfather participated in the decision to place him for adoption, and what his feelings were about his child. The reaction of many parents to this need is: "But I don't *know*."

Overcoming a lack of information

Adoptive parents often have little factual information about their child's biologic father and know even less about his emotional reaction to being a birthfather, although more of an effort is being made to obtain this information.

Contributors to a sperm bank are treated impersonally. Sperm is sometimes "mixed," and may include the sperm of the husband thought to be infertile so that positive paternity can only be determined with sophisticated testing. Records are seldom kept to establish identity of the biologic father.

Fathers themselves have not been very vocal about their feelings. Men are not expected to be nurturers, so they may not be comfortable talking about their feelings toward the children they never knew or are separated from. They may also believe it is useless to express their feelings about their children when "father's rights" are given so little attention. It's only been since 1976 that the birthfather has had any legal right to be consulted about a woman's decision to place her baby for adoption. But too often, the agency, doctor, or lawyer facilitating the adoption makes only a feeble attempt to contact the birthfather. It is much easier to list him as "unknown."

Avoiding stereotypes

When people have inaccurate or incomplete information, they often arrive at incorrect conclusions. We assume that if a birthfather knew about the pregnancy or child, his absence indicates his lack of concern. If he didn't "stay around long enough" to know about the pregnancy, that is also considered evidence of lack of concern. Thus, a stereotype has developed of birthfathers as uninvolved and unconcerned. That kind of attitude does them and our children a disservice.

It is more accurate to think of birthfathers as caring individuals who may not have been given an opportunity to express their feelings about their children.

We shouldn't assume that because the birthfather wasn't still involved with the birthmother at the time of the pregnancy that he didn't care about her. Sexual activity places a stress on a relationship that can contribute to its breakdown. Pregnancy is one more stress. A man may also feel that if he doesn't intend to marry the woman who is carrying his child, he has no right to continue to be involved with her. These are the feelings of sensitive, rather than insensitive, men.

Even the man who stays involved with the birthmother through her pregnancy (but doesn't plan to marry her) is seldom involved in deciding what to do about the pregnancy.

One birthfather told me he felt so guilty that his girlfriend was going through more than he was as a result of their actions that he didn't believe he had a right to make any decisions about his child if he wasn't willing to marry his girlfriend. While it might have appeared to the casual observer that he went off to college and let the birthmother deal with the pregnancy by herself, he spent the next twenty years providing the birthmother with emotional, physical, and financial support in an attempt to make up for her suffering.

The caring birthfather

Rather than not caring about their children, birthfathers often have many of the same feelings about their children that birthmothers have. While we often hear this from birthfathers in the forefront of the adoption reform movement, I've talked to other birthfathers who have said they wonder what their biologic children are like and how they are getting along.

Social worker Reuben Pannor, who studied birthfathers in the early 1970s, said birthfathers feel guilty that they are not taking more responsibility for their children. They feel grief at the loss of their children, but may be reluctant to call attention to their needs because they see themselves as having "gotten off easy" because they weren't the ones who were pregnant. These, too, are the feelings of sensitive, rather than insensitive, men.

In talking with your child about his birthfather, be honest about what you know while at the same time presenting that information in an understanding way. And if you don't know a lot and must fill in with what is "probably" the case, recognize that our stereotype of the uncaring, uninterested birthfather is *not* "probably" the case. More likely he was a sensitive man who, like the birthmother, was overwhelmed by the situation he was in, who probably wanted to be more involved but thought he wasn't entitled to be, and who probably thinks about his child and wonders about his child's welfare.

Parent: "Do you ever think about what your birthfather might be like?"

Child: "I think he's a mean man who didn't care about me."

Parent: "Why do you think that?"

Child: "I don't know. I just have always thought he must be mean."

Parent: "I think he must have been a nice man or your

birthmother wouldn't have wanted to be close to him the way she did."

Child: "Yeah, I guess."

Parent: "Why do you think he didn't care about you?"

Child: "If he cared about me he would have married my birthmother, and then she could have kept me."

Parent: "Your birthmother made an adoption plan for you because she wasn't grown up enough to take care of a baby. It's easier for two people to take care of a baby than one person, but both of them still need to be grown up."

Child: "Was my birthfather grown up?"

Parent: "We don't know much about him, but probably the reason your birthparents didn't get married was because they both realized they weren't grown up enough to make the important decisions that married people and parents have to make. I think your birthfather is probably sad that he couldn't take care of a baby, just like your birthmother is sad that she couldn't take care of a baby, but is happy that you are with parents who can take care of you."

Child: "Why doesn't he send me letters like my birthmother does?"

Parent: "I don't know. Perhaps nobody told him he could."

Discussing the biologic father in donor insemination

You have probably explained donor insemination to your child by saying that sometimes a doctor takes the sperm from another man and places it into the vagina of the woman using a kind of syringe. Sometime in the middle years, your child may be curious about why you used donor insemination, how the doctor obtains the sperm, and whose sperm it was.

Child: "Why did the doctor use somebody else's sperm?

Why couldn't he use yours?"

Parent: "My body wasn't working correctly, so the sperm I made weren't healthy enough to make a baby."

Child: "Whose sperm did the doctor use? His own?"

Parent: "I don't know whose sperm it was, but it wasn't the doctor's. The doctor knew a man who wanted to help people like us who want children but can't make them because the husband can't make enough healthy sperm. The doctor took sperm from this man and placed it in mommy's vagina with a syringe. One of those sperm fertilized one of mommy's eggs and grew into you."

Child: "How'd he get the sperm?"

Parent: "Men and women are able to stimulate themselves to the point of orgasm. For a man, orgasm involves the release of semen which contains sperm. This can be collected and used immediately, or it can be frozen until it is needed for donor insemination."

Child: "Does the doctor know whose sperm it was?"

Parent: "He might. Usually they don't keep any records. They're afraid that we might ask your biologic father for money to help raise you, but we wouldn't do that. The doctor might remember who the biologic father is, but he might not tell us because he promised the biologic father that he wouldn't. I think you should be allowed to find out who your biologic father is if you want to know, but I don't know if you would be able to. Your biologic father might wonder sometimes whether his sperm was ever used and what kind of child grew from his sperm, but he might not be able to find out about you, either."

In talking about donor insemination, it's perhaps easier to talk about sperm than it is the man who donated the sperm. It's important that the biologic father in donor insemination be presented to the child as a real and caring person.

One birthfather told me that he began making donations for infertile couples as a way to earn money for college and didn't think much at first about the outcome of his efforts. Gradually, however, he began to realize that he was helping to create children.

Once, when he went to the doctor to make a donation, he noticed that the chart of the woman who was to receive his sperm was open on the table. He wrote down her name and address and the name of the hospital she would be using for the pregnancy. He planned to contact the hospital in nine months to see if the woman had delivered a baby and invent an excuse to look through the nursery window. "I wanted to know what a child of mine would look like," he said. He never carried through with his plan because he wasn't sure how he would explain his interest to the hospital personnel.

This biologic father says he tries not to think about the children that have resulted from his sperm donations: "When I play with my nieces and nephews, I'm thinking that someone I don't know is playing with my kids the way I'm playing with my nieces and nephews. I try not to think about it because it upsets me that I have no contact with these people."

One final point should be made in discussing donor insemination. Be sure to explain that an inability to produce sperm does not affect the ability to make love. Children this age are beginning to be concerned about their own reproductive ability, and children shouldn't worry about being sterile or impotent.

Lesbian women and donor insemination

If you are a lesbian woman who chose donor insemination, you have to decide when it is appropriate to explain to your child your sexual orientation. If you do not believe your child is ready for that information, you can explain that while you wanted a baby, you were not in love with a man and didn't think you would ever be in love with a man. And you didn't feel comfortable (or didn't feel it was "right") making love with a man if you didn't love him. You can explain that a doctor placed the sperm in your vagina using a syringe, or that a friend placed the sperm in your vagina using a syringe or a turkey baster.

Stepparent adoptions

When there has been an adoption by a stepparent, the biologic mother may have her own feelings about the birthfather that may get in the way of discussing him positively. She needs to separate her feelings about his behavior from his value as a human being. A woman might be perfectly justified being angry at a man who abandoned her when he found out she was pregnant and who has never inquired about the welfare of their child. But it's important to look for the qualities about the man that she found pleasing enough to become sexually involved with him.

Mother: "Your father was an athletic man who enjoyed being around people, but who wasn't ready to take on the responsibilities of being a parent. It scared him to think about having to take care of a wife and a baby. Sometimes, when things scare us, we run away from them. Have you ever run away from something you were scared would be too hard for you?"

Child: "I'm pretty scared when we take math tests at school, but you can't run away from them."

Mother: "But do you want to run away?"

Child: "Oh, yeah."

Mother: "Do you ever put off doing your math homework because you're scared it will be too hard for you?"

Child: "Sometimes."

Mother: "That's probably a lot like the way your father felt—that being a father would be too hard and he wouldn't do it as well as he wanted to."

Child: "Why doesn't he ever call me or write to me?"

Mother: "Maybe he's embarrassed that he ran away from something because it was hard. Or maybe he thinks I'll be angry at him for running away. Or maybe he thinks you'll be angry at him for running away. But I would bet that even though he has never called or written, he wonders about you—what you're like, what you look like, and what you think about him."

One mother was distressed that her children had been abandoned by not only their birthfather, but by the stepfather who had adopted them. After the mother and stepfather were divorced, he refused to pay child support or have any contact with the children, saying they "weren't really his."

This example illustrates why parents should carefully examine their motives before a stepparent adopts a child, and make sure the stepparent is adopting the child out of love and commitment and not to please his wife or prove his commitment to the relationship. If such a situation does occur, children need to be reassured that the problem is the parent's and not theirs:

Child: "Why doesn't Bill ever call me?"

Parent: "How do you feel about his not calling?"

Child: "I don't know."

Parent: "I think I might feel angry, if I were in your place."

Child: "Sometimes it makes me angry. I've left messages on his answering machine but he never calls me back. And he promised to take me to a football game and he never did. But it's stupid of me to think he'd want to go somewhere with me."

Parent: "What makes you say that?"

Child: "Well, it's not like he's my real father or anything."

Parent: "I think Bill's missing an awful lot by not doing things with you. When Bill and I were married I noticed that he would sometimes promise people things because he wanted to make them happy, but sometimes they were promises he shouldn't have made because he knew when he made them that he couldn't keep them. Then, when he can't keep his promise, he gets embarrassed and doesn't want to be around the people he made promises to. I think Bill's embarrassed that he promised to be your father and he wasn't really ready to be your father, so he's embarrassed to talk to you or see you."

Explaining difficult situations

Whenever I speak to adoptive parents I'm asked how much children should be told about biologic parents who made an adoption plan or whose parental rights were terminated as a result of substance abuse, child abuse, incest, rape, mental illness, abandonment, or some other situation that is difficult to explain.

Try to explain situations that seem beyond a child's comprehension by finding a comparable experience the child may have had. Be clear that the adult is responsible for the situation, not the child. Separate the birthparents' behavior from their inherent value as human beings so that the behavior can be condemned without the birthparents being condemned, too. Remember, your child feels a real connection to his birthparents—indeed, is genetically connected to them. If he feels his birthparents were bad people, he may feel he is bad, too.

In discussing involuntary termination of parental rights with a child, pediatrician Vera Fahlberg recommends telling the child that his parents were asking for help, but didn't know how to ask for it verbally, so they gave other signals that the family needed help. As a result of these signals, somebody else saw that the child needed and deserved to grow in ways that the birthparents couldn't provide. Children often have experienced being afraid or unwilling to admit they need help, which can be useful in helping them understand why their birthparents didn't ask for help verbally. They can also be helped to see that because they have had other parents, they have choices their birthparents may not have had. For example, they may have learned ways to express anger that their birthparents did not have the opportunity to learn.

Alcoholism and substance abuse

Child: "Why didn't my birthparents keep me?"

Parent: "Do you remember anything about when you lived with your birthparents?"

Child: "Not very much."

Parent: "Do you remember that you sometimes had to get your own dinner, and that you sometimes had to go to the grocery store by yourself?"

Child: "I remember doing that sometimes."

Parent: "Do you know how old you were then?"

Child: "I guess I was about five."

Parent: "That's right. Do you think most five-year-olds fix their own dinner and go to the grocery store by themselves?"

Child: "No."

Parent: "It isn't a good decision to let a five-year-old go to the grocery store by himself. Your birthparents weren't making good decisions about you because they were drinking too much (or using drugs). They weren't making very good decisions about themselves, either."

Child: "Why didn't they stop?"

Parent: "They probably wanted to stop, but it isn't that easy to stop drinking (or using drugs). Sometimes even doctors can't help somebody stop drinking (or using drugs)."

Child: "If they loved me they would have stopped and taken care of me."

Parent: "I don't know why they didn't stop, but I don't

think it had anything to do with how much they loved you. Eventually, other people noticed that you weren't being taken care of the way you needed to be, and they decided to place you with parents who could make good decisions about you so that you would grow up the way children deserve to grow up."

Physical abuse

Child: "You stole me from my real parents."

Parent: "What makes you say that?"

Child: "My real parents wanted to keep me and you took me away from them."

Parent: "I'm sure your birthparents wanted to keep you, but they also realized they were doing things that hurt you, and that you deserved to live in a family where you wouldn't get hurt. They didn't know how to ask somebody for help, so they gave some signals that they needed help."

Child: "Like what?"

Parent: "Sometimes when they hit you, they hit you in places where people could see the bruises. That's one way people let other people know their child is being hurt and needs help. It might have been better for you if they could have just asked for help, but I guess they didn't know how to do that."

Child: "Why didn't they just stop hitting me?"

Parent: "Why do you think they didn't stop hitting you?"

Child: "I guess because I kept being bad."

Parent: "What did you do that was so bad?"

Child: "I don't know."

Parent: "Don't you remember doing anything bad?"

Child: "No. What did I do?"

Parent: "Usually when children do something that deserves punishment, they remember what it is. Do you remember when you broke into the school last year?"

Child: "Yeah."

Parent: "That was something unacceptable, wasn't it?"

Child: "Yeah."

Parent: "Do you remember what the consequences of that were?

Child: "Yes. Don't remind me."

Parent: "Okay. When you do something unacceptable, get caught, and have to deal with the consequences, you remember what happened. I think that the reason you don't remember what you did that got you beaten was that you weren't doing anything wrong. I think you were just acting like a child. The reason you got beaten was that your birthmother got out of control when she got angry. When you get angry, do you ever want to hit somebody or something?"

Child: "Yeah. Sometimes I do."

Parent: "Well, that's probably how your birthmother felt. But adults aren't supposed to hit children."

Child: "Then why did she?"

Parent: "Probably her parents hit her when they were angry, so she never learned other ways to express her anger. You didn't know any other ways to express your anger when you came to live with us. That's why you hit a lot, and why sometimes you still do. But you're learning other ways, aren't you?"

Child: "Yeah. Sometimes I go outside and kick a soccer ball, and I kick it really hard."

Parent: "And just now you said what you were angry about. That's another way people express their anger. You said you thought we stole you. And you sounded angry about that."

Child: "I was."

Parent: "I can understand that you're angry that you had to be separated from your birthparents, and that you had to live with foster families for two years before you

were adopted. I would also understand if you were
angry that your birthparents hit you."

Child: "I am. It hurt."

Parent: "Of course it hurt. Your birthmother was bigger
than you. I don't think she wanted to hurt you, but she
just didn't know how to stop. So she gave some signs
that brought the fact that you were hurting to the
attention of people who could see that you got the help
you needed and deserved."

Sexual abuse

Children who were sexually abused often feel responsible
for the abuse happening. And when they tried to stop the
abuse by telling somebody about it, it sometimes seems to
them like they were punished for telling by having to leave the
family. Those feelings might be revealed by a situation such
as this one:

Parent: "Why didn't you tell me you broke the window?"

Child: "Because if you do something bad and you tell, you
have to go away."

Parent: "You mean, go to jail?"

Child: "No, just go away."

Parent: "I don't understand. Have you ever had to go
away because you did something bad and told someone
about it?"

Child: "Yes. That's why I had to come here."

Parent: "You had to leave your birth family and come
here because your birthparents weren't taking care of
you in the way that you needed and deserved."

Child: "What do you mean?"

Parent: "Your birthfather was touching you in ways that
are okay for an adult to touch another adult, but aren't
okay for an adult to touch a child. He probably knew it
wasn't okay for him to do that and he probably gave

you clues that he knew it wasn't okay by telling you not to tell anyone what he was doing."

Child: "Why did he do it if he knew it wasn't okay?"

Parent: "He probably wanted to be close to you. When you want to be close to someone, what do you like to do?"

Child: "Sit on their lap. Hug them."

Parent: "Sure. And that's okay. But your birthfather wanted to be close in ways that aren't okay. And you knew it wasn't okay because you told your teacher about it so that she would help you stop your birthfather from touching you in those ways."

Child: "I shouldn't have told her. I should have just made him stop."

Parent: "You probably told your teacher because you couldn't make him stop by yourself. Children aren't supposed to be able to take care of themselves. You did the right thing by asking her to help you. What happened when you told your teacher?"

Child: "My mom got mad at me, and I had to leave."

Parent: "I think your birthmother was mad at herself for not stopping your birthfather from touching you. And I think she was mad at your birthfather, too. Sometimes I yell at you when I'm really mad about something else, don't I?"

Child: "Sometimes."

Parent: "That's not fair, but it happens sometimes. What I think happened when you told your teacher what your birthfather was doing is that she and some other people saw that you weren't being taken care of in your birth family the way you needed to be. They saw that you came to a family who could help you grow and change in the ways you deserve."

Rape, incest and prostitution

In discussing the reason a birthmother made an adoption

plan for a child conceived as a result of rape, incest, or prostitution, keep a discussion of the child's conception separate from a discussion of the adoption plan. In most cases, the child seven to eleven years old is not ready to hear about such details. (How to talk to a teenager about a birthmother who was a prostitute or a biologic father who was a rapist is discussed in Chapter 6.)

Even in cases of rape, incest, and prostitution, the reason the birthmother placed the child for adoption is still her inability at that point in her life to care for a baby. Perhaps she is unable to care for a baby because of the psychological trauma of rape or incest. Perhaps her life as a prostitute is an indication of her inability to make good decisions about herself and those she cares about, or to take care of herself and those she cares about. The important point is that the child not think he was rejected as a result of the way he was conceived.

In discussing the biologic father in these situations, concentrate on providing information that will not later be contradicted by the facts. If you discuss the rape or incest at all, be sure to distinguish between the biologic father's behavior and his value as a human being.

Child: "Why didn't my birthmother keep me?"

Parent: "You were born at a time in your birthmother's life when it was taking all her concentration to take care of herself and the children she already had. She couldn't take care of any new baby then."

Child: "Why didn't my biologic father help her?"

Parent: "She wasn't married to your biologic father."

Child: "Couldn't he help her anyway?"

Parent: "I don't think he knew about you."

Child: "Why didn't she tell him?"

Parent: "I don't think she knew where he was."

Child: "Why didn't she try to find him?"

Parent: "I think she didn't like the way he behaved
sometimes, so she didn't want to be around him."

Child: "What didn't she like?"

Parent: "He didn't always respect her feelings. He might
want to do something that she didn't want to do, and he
would make her do it anyway."

The parent might want to ask the child if he knows
anyone who insists on having his own way. Most children
have some experience with children who threaten or bully
others so that they can have their own way.

Mental illness or mental retardation

While mental illness, like alcoholism and drug abuse, is
considered a "disease," take care that you don't give the child
the impression that when parents are "sick," the children have
to go away. Concentrate instead on the fact that the birthparents were unable to take care of themselves and their
children, or make good decisions for themselves and their
children.

Child: "Why couldn't my birthmother take care of a
baby?"

Parent: "To take care of a baby, you have to be grown up
so you can make decisions that will help your child
grow properly. Your birthmother's body was grown up,
but her mind was not grown up and it never would be.
She still needed someone to take care of her, so she
couldn't take care of any baby."

Child: "Who takes care of her?"

Parent: "She lives in a house with other people who also
need help taking care of themselves. Some people who
can help them take care of themselves live with them."

Child: "Why couldn't they take care of me, too?"

Parent: "It isn't always the same people who take care of
your birthmother and the people she lives with.

Children need and deserve parents who care about
them and who can take care of them."

The disabled child

Children who are physically or mentally disabled may
believe they were "rejected" by their birthparents because of
their disability. In some cases, birthparents do place children
for adoption because they are not prepared to take care of a
child with disabilities. Parents can explain that in a way that
does not make the child feel responsible by emphasizing – but
not condemning – the birthparents' lack of ability.

Child: "I bet my birthmother would have kept me if I
wasn't in a wheelchair."

Parent: "Not everyone knows how to take care of someone in a wheelchair. Maybe your birthmother was afraid
that she wouldn't do a good job taking care of you, and
she knew you deserved to be well taken care of."

The child with serious behavior problems

We don't want children to think they were placed for
adoption because they were "bad," yet sometimes children are
placed for adoption because their biologic parents cannot control the children's behavior.

Children who set fires, hurt animals or other children, run
away, or have other serious behavior problems should be held
accountable for their actions. But a lot of children behave in
these ways who are not placed for adoption. The difference is
that some parents are better able than others to deal with difficult behavior.

Parent: "Do you know why your birthmother made an
adoption plan for you?"

Child: "Because I was bad."

Parent: "What did you do that was so bad?"

Child: "I set a fire in the basement."

Parent: "How do you think your birthmother felt when she saw the basement on fire?"

Child: "She was scared."

Parent: "How do you think she felt after the fire was put out?"

Child: "I don't know."

Parent: "I think maybe she was scared in a different way. She was scared because she could see that if you were setting fires you needed help and she didn't know how to give you the help you needed. So she found a way to see that you had parents who could give you the help she didn't know how to give."

Building the adoption story

Children mature a great deal between the ages of seven and eleven. The story you tell the eleven-year-old is going to be much more detailed than the story you tell a child four years younger. By anticipating this, you can build a story that you can add to as your child's ability to understand the details increases without misleading your child or contradicting yourself.

For example, if a child had been abandoned in a gas station restroom shortly after birth, the parent of that young child might discuss the situation this way:

Parent: "We don't know much about your birthmother. We think she was probably very young. Probably when you were born she saw how tiny babies are and she realized how much help babies need to grow and change the way they are supposed to. She probably decided she didn't know enough about taking care of babies to take care of one."

Later on, the parent can expand the story, still leaving out the fact that the child was abandoned.

Child: "Was I born in a hospital?"

Parent: "No, you weren't. We don't know for sure, but it seems that your birthmother was so young she didn't even know she was going to have a baby. Or maybe she was scared because she knew she didn't know how to take care of babies, so she pretended she wasn't going to have one. So, when it was time for you to be born, she didn't go to the hospital. Most babies are strong and healthy and don't need to be in a hospital when they're born, but most mothers go to the hospital just in case they or their babies have problems when they're born. We're glad you were healthy and didn't need hospital care."

When the child is mature enough to hear about the abandonment, the parent can say:

Parent: "You were probably born at home. Your birthmother was probably scared because she didn't know how to take care of a baby, and maybe she thought people would be angry with her because she had a baby, so she tried to hide you. Have you ever hidden something because you were afraid someone would be angry with you?"

Child: "I broke Michael's skateboard and hid it, but he found it."

Parent: "And someone found you, too, because your birthmother didn't hide you very well. I think she really wanted someone to find you so that you'd be taken care of, but she didn't want anyone to know that she was the one who had hidden you."

Child: "Where did she hide me?"

Parent: "She went to a gas station and tried to hide you in the restroom. But, of course, you cried, and someone in the gas station heard you and found you right away."

Child: "You mean she just left me in the restroom?"

Parent: "Uh-huh. How does that make you feel?"

Child: "She must not have cared about me at all."

Parent: "I think she probably cared about you, and probably wanted to go back and find out if you were okay. But she was scared. That doesn't mean it was okay for her to do that. It wasn't. It wasn't the way to take care of a baby. But I think your birthmother was scared and didn't know any other way to ask for help."

Parents ask me how much detail they should provide their children about situations such as abandonment, abuse, and mental illness. It seems they want to provide their children with just the minimum amount of unpleasant information so that their children aren't needlessly hurt. That's understandable, but it may also not be in the child's best interests. Sometimes the details that are the most painful are the ones that make everything else in the story make sense. While there may be occasional exceptions, in general I believe children should have all available information about them by the time they leave home. How much they are told before that time depends on their intellectual and emotional maturity, but they do need to have enough information to help them work through the different questions they have at different stages of development.

Whenever parents provide their children with unpleasant information about the past, they should make sure they are available to provide emotional support to the child who may feel sad, angry, or ashamed. If necessary, a therapist may be needed to help the child sort out his emotional reactions to information about his past.

Answering other questions about adoption

Children in the middle years are busy gathering information about themselves, their families, and their world. It is a time of discovery. In thinking about their birthparents, they are likely to have questions about what the birthparents looked like, their abilities, and their personalities. They may wonder if their birthparents were married and what being born to unmarried parents says about them. They may be interested in knowing if they have any siblings or half-siblings.

Parents who have easy access to more information about their children's birthparents may want to take advantage of that opportunity before their children reach adolescence. Those who don't have more information readily available may want to make the extra effort necessary to obtain more information at this time. The need for more details about the birthparents may not seem as urgent during middle childhood as it will in adolescence, but the more the school-age child is able to have his questions answered, the easier it will be for him to make sense of being adopted. Furthermore, because the need of the teenager is so urgent and it may take time to obtain the information, it's only prudent to start early.

Sharing mementos

Parents have asked me when they should show their children photographs of the birth family or share other memorabilia or information with their children. The child in the middle childhood years is likely to ask some questions or express an interest in his birthparents that would naturally lead to sharing this kind of material with him. If not, you may choose to share the material as a way of drawing out your child on these issues.

For example, many adoptive families today have letters written by their children's birthmothers explaining their reasons for placing their children for adoption. These letters tend to be tender, moving accounts of the birthmothers' feelings – expressions of love that help children understand why they were placed for adoption. I would read such a letter to a child as part of his adoption story – even before he could fully understand it. By the time he reached the middle childhood years, I'd see that he had a copy that he could keep and read whenever he chose to (keeping the original in a safe deposit box).

Parents don't need to wait for a "special occasion" to share with their children letters, a good-bye gift from the birthmother, or photos of the birth family. The "right moment" to share such material is when a child needs it, and not on a "special occasion." This material belongs to the child – it is not a gift from you. Furthermore, if adoption is discussed in the family as a matter of course, whenever it seems appropriate, you may find that the "right moment" to show your child the sweater his birthmother crocheted for him is when you are cleaning out the closet and come across the box with the sweater in it.

Birthparent fantasies

One ten-year-old boy, who held his class record in the one-mile run, watched the Olympics on television and suggested to his parents that perhaps one of the athletes competing in the track and field events was his birthfather.

Such fantasies about the birthparents are not uncommon at this age. Psychiatrists since Sigmund Freud have talked about "family romance fantasies" in which children imagine they are adopted. Often this is explained as children's reaction to parental behavior that they don't like. They think their "real" parents would let them do what they want, wouldn't get angry at their behavior, and would otherwise be ideal. Psychologist David Elkind explains such fantasies as a way for children in middle childhood – who are discovering that their parents are not perfect – to explain why they are so much smarter than their parents. They couldn't have been born to such stupid people, they reason; they must have been adopted.

But while nonadopted children can manipulate their adoption fantasies to meet their emotional needs, children who are adopted may find the facts of their adoption conflicting with what they would like to believe.

> Parent: "Why do you think your birthfather is an Olympic athlete?"
>
> Child: "Well, I'm a good runner. Probably one of my birthparents was a good runner."
>
> Parent: "I wouldn't be surprised. Of course, there are a lot of good runners who never make it to the Olympics."
>
> Child: "I know. It would just be neat if he was."
>
> Parent: "It would be neat, but it isn't likely. Do you know how old your birthfather is now?"
>
> Child: "No."
>
> Parent: "He was twenty-two when you were born, so he'd be how old now?"
>
> Child: "Thirty."
>
> Parent: "That's right. Now there are some Olympic athletes who are thirty years old, but not many."

It's normal for children to imagine that their birthparents are famous, rich, or otherwise more attractive than their adoptive parents. Parents can remind their children of facts about the birthparents that contradict the fantasy, or provide general information about adoption that argues against the likelihood of their parents being rich and famous, even though such evidence is unlikely to convince a child who wants to believe otherwise. But fantasizing about the birthparents is part of normal development and continues into adolescence. If the child becomes preoccupied with the fantasies, professional help in sorting out fantasy from reality may be necessary.

Identifying the birthparents

Children in middle childhood are likely to want to know who their birthparents are. Children who have contact with their birthparents shouldn't be misled about their identities. For example, grandparents who adopt their daughter's child should make it clear what the biologic relationships in the family are. Without this honesty, the child is likely to grow up knowing that there's a family secret and may hear the truth in an undesirable way.

Parents who know the identity of their child's birthparents but do not have regular contact with them, or who could easily learn the identity of the birthparents, should consider the advantage of sharing this information during their child's elementary school years rather than waiting until adolescence. Once children learn who their birthparents are, they are likely at some point to want to meet them. Establishing contact with the birth family during the middle childhood years may be easier than in adolescence because the family has time to sort out the expectations and roles of everyone involved in the adoption while children are still accepting of having parents in their lives. And in the process, children gain access to a lot of information they need to answer their immediate questions.

As we discuss in Chapters 6 and 7, it can be confusing to the teenager to meet a new set of parents at a time when the teenager is trying to establish independence from his parents.

(For more about having contact with birthparents during middle childhood, see "Open adoptions," later in this chapter.)

The child's interest in names

The preschooler may be confused by the idea that he had one first name before he was adopted and got a new first name after he was adopted. He may think he was one person before he was adopted and literally became a different person after the adoption. Or, until he understands that a person can be both good and bad at the same time, he may think one name is his "bad person" and the other is his "good person." However, the school-age child is more likely to understand that his first name was changed when he was adopted and be interested in what his original name was and why it was changed.

When she was almost nine, my daughter asked me why we hadn't kept her Korean name. I replied that we didn't think to keep part of her Korean name. (Although I've since come to the conclusion that keeping a child's original name as part of her new name – perhaps as a middle name – is an important part of recognizing her heritage, especially for a foreign-born child, it didn't occur to my husband and me when we first adopted.) My daughter, who has a rather common name, said she thought it would be "neat" to have an unusual name at school. I explained that we thought she might be teased at school if she had an unusual name. She said that when she grew up she was going to be known by her Korean name. I told her that would be fine.

At a workshop I gave, an adoptive father expressed concern that his son, who was in the second grade, wanted to be known by his middle name instead of by his first name, which was the same as his father's. Many children go through a stage when they want to spell their names differently or be known by another name – often their middle name. This is only harmful if it reflects a belief by the child that he will really be a different person if he has a different name. In adolescence, changing a name or changing the spelling of a name may be a way for a teenager to experiment with different identities, which is a normal part of development. And a teenage boy who is adopted may have difficulty being "junior" to a father who seems quite different from the way he sees himself. (The difficulty adolescent adoptees have in forming an identity is discussed in Chapter 6.) Whether a child wants to change his name as a whim or because he has difficulty identifying with the father whose name he shares, it's generally a request parents can honor.

Discussing adoption costs

The child who was adopted as a result of a surrogate

arrangement, a private adoption, or donor insemination may focus on the financial transaction that took place between his adoptive parents and his birthparents, and conclude that his birthparents were motivated by money. No doubt you would never give your child this impression yourself, but if you have never discussed the financial aspects of adoption with your child, he may be unprepared to interpret the financial transaction on his own or if someone at school taunts him with it. So anticipate this happening sometime during the school years, and when you talk about adoption, put the financial aspects in their proper perspective.

Child: "Did you have to pay for me?"

Parents: "It's against the law to buy or sell people. We didn't pay for you, but there are always costs involved in adding someone to a family. Can you think of some of them?"

Child: "You have to pay the doctor."

Parent: "And you have to pay the hospital. What else?"

Child: "You have to buy clothes for the baby and baby food."

Parent: "After the baby is born, yes. But even before the baby is born the mother needs different clothes to wear while she's pregnant. It's important for her to eat healthy foods and drink lots of milk. Some women aren't able to work when they're pregnant so they need extra money to pay their bills. We thought that since your birthmother was going to place you with us after you were born, it was only right for us to pay those expenses. Plus, it cost money for the social worker and the attorney who helped us adopt you."

Child: "How much did all that cost?"

Parent: "It cost a lot, but we didn't care because we were so happy to have you."

Child: "I bet my birthmother was happy to get all that money, though."

Parent: "I'm sure it relieved her to know we would help her with her expenses. But I'm sure it didn't make her feel any less sad at being separated from you."

Birthmothers involved in adoption through surrogacy and biologic fathers involved in adoption through donor insemination have told me that the money they received, which may sound substantial, was not a motivating factor so much as compensation for their inconvenience. Biologic fathers cite expenses such as lost time from work and the inconvenience of being "on call" to deliver a sperm donation to a clinic whenever the woman who was to receive it was ovulating. Birthmothers point out that there are easier ways to make money than by carrying a baby for nine months. But they feel they – and their families – deserve compensation for the time and effort it took not just to carry the baby, but to conceive, which may take several months.

Open adoptions

It isn't unusual for the amount of contact between the birth family and the adoptive family to vary greatly during the first few years of a child's life. The birthmother often wants a lot of contact during the first year of the child's life, but once reassured that the child is growing well in a loving family, she may put some distance between her and the adoptive family as she proceeds with the life that was interrupted by the pregnancy. Contact at that time may be primarily with the birth grandparents. Later, as the birthmother becomes more settled, she may become more actively involved with the adoptive family than she had been, although not as involved as she was during the child's first year.

By the time the child reaches school age, the adoptive family and the birth family generally have established a regular routine and have clarified their roles. Social workers who facilitate open adoptions tell me that the birthmother often functions as a close friend of the adoptive parents, who, like other close friends, is interested in the welfare of the children in the family. But she does not try to function as a parent.

Birthfathers haven't been as involved in open adoptions as birthmothers because, as noted earlier in this chapter, they tend to be left out of the adoption decision and process. But sometimes, after they have married and had a family, birthfathers attempt to re-establish contact with the child who was placed for adoption. So the birthfather may become involved in an open adoption during the child's elementary school years.

The main benefit of open adoptions to children this age is that they have easy access to answers to their many questions. Adoptive parents don't have to guess whether the birthparents ever married each other, what kinds of jobs they now have, or whether the adopted child has any full or half-siblings, for example. Most important, open adoptions provide an opportunity for the birthparents to explain directly to the child why he was placed for adoption.

While open adoptions generally proceed smoothly, they do present some unique situations.

Children's responsibility in open adoptions

The mother of a nine-year-old boy was concerned that her son didn't want to send his birthmother a Mother's Day card. At a workshop session, she asked if she should insist that he send her a card, buy one for him to sign, or ignore the occasion. Another mother wondered whether she should continue to correspond with the birth family when her ten-year-old daughter seemed uninterested in the letters she received from her birthmother.

Because open adoptions are arranged for the benefit of the children, parents may think that if the children don't seem interested in having contact with the birthparents, there's no need to continue the relationship. In fact, the agreement to have contact in an open adoption is made between the adults involved. Parents have a responsibility to live up to that agreement regardless of whether the child wants to take an active role in the relationship or not.

Children go through stages in which they are less interested in adoption and their birthparents than they are at other times. Sometimes they want to ignore their adoption so they can feel more like their friends who are not adopted. Sometimes children avoid anything having to do with adoption because they don't want to confront some troubling issues. They also sometimes resist doing something just because their parents want them to do it.

Parents can try to draw children out on their reasons for not wanting to have contact with their birth families, in case the children are avoiding a particular issue that needs to be addressed. However, if children really don't want to write or talk to a birth relative, I don't think they should be forced to or feel guilty for not doing so. Parents can continue to keep the relationship open for those times when the child is interested.

Most adoptive parents feel comfortable with an open adoption after a few years. But if children are avoiding contact with their birth relatives, it could be because they have received a message that the parents feel hurt or rejected when the children have contact with their birth families. Parents should analyze their own feelings about open adoptions to make sure this isn't at the root of the children's reluctance to communicate with the birth relatives.

The birthparent whose interest diminishes

It surprises some people to learn that the chief complaint of adoptive parents in open adoptions is that the birth families aren't as involved as the adoptive families would like them to be. As their children grow and develop an increasing awareness of adoption, adoptive parents recognize the benefit of having access to information about the birthparents.

However, birthparents tend to be younger than adoptive parents and are busy completing their education, establishing careers, developing new relationships, and having families. They may need a lot of contact with the children they placed for adoption during times of emotional crisis, but may not be as involved at other times as the adoptive families would like.

Parents can deal with their children's feelings where their expectations are not realized by: allowing them to express their feelings, affirming their right to feel as they do, and explaining the birthparents' behavior without excusing or condemning it.

Parent: "You seem sad. Was there something about your birthday party that disappointed you?"

Child: "No, not really."

Parent: "It seems to me that you are disappointed about something."

Child: "It's stupid."

Parent: "I bet it's not stupid. Would you like to tell me about it?"

Child: "I thought I might get at least a card from my birthmother."

Parent: "I'd be disappointed, too, if I expected a card from my birthmother and didn't get it. Why do you suppose she didn't send one?"

Child: "She probably forgot."

Parent: "I find it hard to believe that she'd forget something so important. Does it seem to you like we haven't heard from her as much this year as we did last year?"

Child: "Yeah. Last year she sent me a present for my birthday and a present for Christmas and she wrote me a lot. But I've only gotten one letter from her this year. I guess she likes her new baby better than she does me."

Parent: "Do you remember what it was like the first year we had Sam?"

Child: "What do you mean?"

Parent: "Well, new babies take a lot of their mom's time and energy, don't they?"

Child: "Yeah."

Parent: "Do you remember feeling jealous when I couldn't play a game with you or read you a book because Sam was crying?"

Child: "Yeah."

Parent: "It was easier for me to see that you were hurt by all the attention Sam was getting because you were right here. Maybe your birthmother doesn't realize how you feel. How would you feel about writing her and telling her that you feel she doesn't care about you as much now that she has a new baby?"

The irresponsible birthparent

Occasionally adoptive families will be involved with birthparents who have difficulty acting responsibly in a relationship. They may act impulsively or erratically, for example, lavishing a child with presents one day and then not calling the child for weeks. Parents in such a situation probably will want to work closely with their adoption facilitator to help the birthparents learn how to participate responsibly in the open adoption relationship. But until they do, their behavior can pose a dilemma for the adoptive parents who understand the importance of children having a positive attitude about their birthparents.

One adoptive mother asked me what she should tell her daughter when she asked who her birthfather is. The birthmother insists that a particular man is the child's birthfather, but the man denies it. While the adoptive mother doesn't have any evidence as to the identity of the birthfather, she doesn't believe that the birthmother is telling the truth—a situation that has occurred before with the birthmother. The adoptive mother anticipates that her desire to be honest with her daughter by telling her she doesn't know who her birthfather is will conflict with the birthmother's story. Yet she doesn't want to be in the position of telling her daughter that her birthmother often lies about important matters.

While her immediate problem may be deciding what to tell her daughter about her birthfather, this is likely to be only one of several occasions in which the family will have to deal with the effects of a birthmother who distorts the truth.

The daughter can be helped to understand that her birthmother makes mistakes sometimes, but that it doesn't make her a bad person.

Child: "Who is my birthfather?"

Parent: "I don't know who your birthfather is."

Child: "Tiffany says Jeff is my birthfather."

Parent: "Tiffany has told me that, too, but I have a difficult time believing that. The first time Tiffany and I discussed your birthfather, she said she didn't know who he was. I think maybe she was embarrassed that she didn't know something that important. She wanted to be able to tell you who your birthfather is because she knows how important it is to you, so she started saying Jeff is your birthfather. After a while she had said it so many times that now she really believes it. Have you ever wanted something to be true so badly that pretty soon you believed it was true?"

Child: "I don't think so."

Parent: "Do you remember the time you told your friend Liza that we were all going to Disney World? You wanted to go to Disney World so badly that pretty soon you believed that we were going."

Child: "I remember.

Grieving for the losses in adoption

Parents are sometimes surprised to find their seven- to eleven-year-old having strong emotional reactions to the way he was conceived or joined his family because he has been so accepting of it in the past. Many parents don't expect their children to react emotionally to being adopted until their adolescent years.

Teenagers often have intense feelings about adoption that are due to their awareness of what has been lost in their lives. But these feelings frequently begin during the middle childhood years. School-age children are seeing themselves, their family, and their situation for the first time in a broader context. They are not just concerned with the technical aspects of family building, but how they are affected by having been adopted. This involves more than whether they are happy or content to be in their families (which they probably are). They also have feelings about being different from the majority of children because they are adopted – feelings which are influenced, in part, by cultural views of family.

Children may react to being adopted sometimes by pretending it happened in a different way, sometimes with anger, sometimes by trying to imagine how the outcome could have been (or could still be) different, and sometimes with sadness. In fact, that range of emotional responses are the typical stages of grief that people go through when they experience a loss. While the actual loss of the birthparents may have occurred some time ago, children in the middle years of childhood are just becoming aware that they have lost someone who played an extremely significant role in their lives.

Even children who have some contact with their birthparents have experienced the loss of them as parental figures in their daily life and consequently are likely to mourn for that loss in some way.

Parents can give children satisfactory answers to their

questions and sensitive responses to their statements and still not spare them painful feelings. But they can comfort them when they're hurting, let them know their feelings are normal, and tell them that they will someday feel better.

Claudia L. Jewett's book *Helping Children Cope with Separation and Loss* (Harvard, Mass.: Harvard Common Press, 1982), is an excellent resource for parents whose children are grieving for an immediate or past loss. While she identifies the stages of grief slightly differently than is done below, the process described is similar.

Denial

One girl asked her adoptive mother, when they were about to move to another city, if when they got to their new home they could pretend she was born to her adoptive mother. Some children may actually carry through with such a pretense at school and with their friends. This may reflect a desire to be more like their peers. They may also be in the denial stage of grief–the stage in which people want to believe that the loss really didn't happen so they won't have to deal with it.

It isn't unusual for children this age to "deny" they were placed for adoption by believing their birthparents were forced into the decision. They might also imagine their adoptive parents stole them–that their birthmothers left them alone for a few minutes, intending to return for them, but before they could, someone found them and thought they had been abandoned. Children adopted through surrogacy might imagine the birthmother changed her mind but was forced to live up to the terms of the surrogate contract.

Should your child share any of these fantasies with you, remember that they don't represent any animosity toward you (the parents who "stole him" from his birthmother) but are a way for him to deal with the pain of his loss. Continue to correct his misunderstandings, but validate his feelings.

Child: "I bet you stole me from the hospital."

Parent: "I know you would like to believe that your birth-mother intended to keep you. I'm sure she wished she could keep you. But she realized that no matter how much she wanted to, it would be better for everyone if you came to live with us. I'm sure that decision was hard for her and made her sad. Sometimes we have to do things even though they make us sad. Do you remember when we moved to this city? We were sad to leave the people we liked in the other town, but we thought it was best for our family to live here."

Child: "I remember my friend Sarah. I still miss her."

Parent: "I know you do."

Anger

Children's anger at having been separated from one or more of their birthparents may be directed at the birthparents or at the adoptive parents. If your child is angry at you, try not to take it as a sign of rejection. Your child may be angry at having been separated from his birthparents even though he may be happy to be in your family.

Parents are most helpful to their children during this stage of grief when they allow them appropriate ways to express their anger. Most people are uncomfortable around angry people even when the anger is under control. Children are often explosive in their expression of anger, which intensifies parents' desire for the children to cool down as soon as possible.

Let your child know that it is all right to feel angry and to express that anger as long as he doesn't hurt himself or other people, or become physically or verbally abusive. For example, he can punch a pillow or punching bag, or scream in the shower. Also give him an opportunity to express what he is angry about.

Bargaining

Bargaining is the last stage of grief in which people believe the loss could still be reversed. They try to reverse the loss by striking a deal with God or fate or whatever power they feel is responsible for their predicament. Children who feel they were placed for adoption because they were "bad" or defective might believe that if they were only perfect, their birthparents would want them back. Ultimately, they realize such bargains are not fulfilled, and the loss is permanent.

Sadness

"I'm sad that I'm not with my birthmother, but if I were with her I wouldn't be with you," said one eight-year-old girl to her adoptive mother.

That statement sums up the feeling many children who have been separated from their birthparents have when they realize what they have lost and that their loss can never be recovered. Unless children remember their birthparent, they probably are not grieving for the loss of a particular person, but are saddened by what we might call a "missed opportunity." But at the same time, they recognize that had they been able to take advantage of that opportunity, they would have missed being with the parents they know and love. The thought of not being with their adoptive parents makes them sad as well.

Children who think they have to decide whether they would rather be with their adoptive parents or with their birthparents are faced with a situation that can only leave them with a loss and, therefore, is unresolvable. Statements like, "Aren't you happy to be with us?" or "If you were in India you would be having a very hard life," send a message to children that they must choose which parents they'd rather be with, and choose their adoptive parents. It's better to respond, "It must be hard to understand why you were adopted," or "It must be sad to be separated from your birthparents."

Children may be reluctant to let their parents know they are feeling sad about being adopted. Children seven to eleven years old are often sensitive enough to know that feeling sad about being adopted may make their parents feel sad, too. Statements such as "I can't tell you why I'm sad," are good clues that a child has some mixed feelings about being adopted. A child might say, "I wish I'd never been adopted." If the child has just had an argument with his parents, he might really wish he had different parents. But if he seems to be expressing his feelings about adoption, parents can try to understand that he's not really expressing dissatisfaction but a weariness at having to deal with issues that are beyond his ability to understand. He probably wishes that his life were simpler, perhaps even that he had been born to both his adoptive parents instead of adopted by them.

Parents who are infertile can probably relate to a child's feelings at this time by remembering the grief they felt each month when their hopes for a pregnancy were dashed. But if those pregnancies had worked out, they would never have had their particular child. Parents can share those feelings with their child:

Child: "I wish my birthmother had kept me, but then I would never have come to live with you."

Parent: "Mommy and daddy tried for a long time to make a baby that would grow inside mommy. We were very sad when we couldn't do it. Then mommy found out she was pregnant. We were so excited. We told all our friends and went out and bought a stroller. Then a sad thing happened. The baby died inside mommy's uterus. We have never been so sad."

Child: "What did you do with the stroller?"

Parent: "We still wanted a baby very much, so we decided to adopt a baby, and that baby was you. I still am sad when I think about the baby who died, but if that baby had been born, we wouldn't have adopted you, and it makes me sad now to think that I would never have known you because I love you so much."

Moving on

While it's difficult to know that your child is hurting and be unable to do anything to ease the pain, remember that out of these stages of grief comes the ability to make sense of what has happened and to move on. This doesn't mean the child understands and accepts everything that has happened to him, but for the time being, he has organized what he knows about his adoption into his life in a meaningful way. He will very likely have to do this again and again as his awareness of adoption changes and deepens.

Some children undoubtedly move through the stages of grief quickly, perhaps imperceptibly. Others may experience a more intense kind of grief. A few may need professional help if they seem to be unable to move from one stage to the next. But if they do not grieve at this time, they will have to grieve later, and later the issues may be more complex because they have lain dormant for so long.

Feelings of insecurity

The child in the middle years is not sophisticated enough to understand the social problems that led to the decisions his birthparents and adoptive parents made. Nor does he have the ability to understand the legal system that guarantees his place in his adoptive family. He does know, however, that children can be separated from their parents. It happened once. It could happen again.

This awareness can make separation more difficult at times for the child who is adopted. For example, when a child starts first grade, it is sometimes the longest separation he has ever had from his mother. His normal anxiety may be intensified by his newly developed understanding of his adoption. Some children are more adaptable than others, and some separate from their mothers more easily. But even a child who is normally easy-going about new situations may have periods of insecurity at this time, depending on how he's dealing with adoption issues. So if a child is suddenly reluctant to spend the night sleeping over at a friend's house, doesn't want to go to camp or even spend a weekend at grandpa's, it may be because he's feeling insecure because of his increased understanding of adoption.

One seven-year-old girl suddenly developed a fear of going to bed at night. "I'm afraid you're going to die in the night, or I'm going to die, or you're not going to be here in the morning," she told her father. No amount of reassurance about the unlikelihood of any of that happening seemed to make any difference. While it didn't appear that her fears had anything to do with adoption, her father suspected that there was a connection. One night he said to her, "I think you're afraid something is going to happen to me because you've already lost your birthparents. I think you're afraid that you're going to lose mommy and me, too. Your birthparents didn't just disappear one night. They couldn't take care of a baby and they made a decision to place you for adoption. They made sure someone else would take care of you. Mommy and I aren't going to disappear either, and we made a decision that we would be your parents." The girl responded, "I don't think that's why I'm afraid." But she was no longer anxious at bedtime.

This father helped his child confront her fears, let her know that he understood them, and reassured her that her place in the family is permanent. If your child is anxious about leaving home, you might allow him some security measures that you might otherwise think he's outgrown. For example, let him telephone you before going to bed at his friend's house, or let him take a transitional object to grandpa's – his old blanket, a stuffed animal, or even something special that belongs to you.

Feelings of inferiority

Children develop a sense of self during middle childhood based on their perceived social status, accomplishments, and abilities. Feelings of inferiority may develop if children get the message that some characteristic, such as gender or religion, is more important than their accomplishments. For example, if society says, "Jews are inferior," children may think that no matter how hard they work or what they accomplish, they will never be as good as other people. Conversely, they may get the message that they are only loved if they achieve success in academics, athletics, or other endeavors.

During these years, adoptees are vulnerable to thinking that because they are adopted they are not as good as other people. Or they may think that they have to be successful to earn their adoptive parents' love or to retain a place in the family. Adoptees are more likely to feel this way if they are told they are "special" because they are adopted or that they were "chosen." They are more likely to develop a positive self-concept if they learn they are loved as unique individuals. While few children will feel popular or successful all the time, persistent feelings of inferiority may require help from a professional.

Groups for children in middle childhood

Recognizing the importance of adoption issues during middle childhood, some adoption agencies are now offering group sessions for "latency-age children" (the term psychologists use to describe children seven to eleven years old). Typically the sessions help parents understand the issues their children are dealing with and give children a chance to explore their feelings. Parents may find their children more receptive to participating in such groups during middle childhood than in adolescence. (For a discussion of how to tell when children need additional help dealing with adoption issues and resources that can be used, see Appendix A: "Do We Need More Help?")

Activity: Making a lifebook

Parents and social workers have found that a good way to help a child share his thoughts and feelings about adoption is to have him make a lifebook. Lifebooks are useful tools to help children organize their memories and make sense of how they joined their families. They traditionally have been used to help a child who has moved from one family to another several times understand his life history.

A lifebook is a chronicle of a child's life. It is a story that begins with his birth, records special events and special people in his life, and provides a place to keep special memories and mementos.

To make a lifebook you will need a scrapbook, art supplies, and a time and place in which you and your child can work without being interrupted.

You'll want your child to draw the illustrations and write the accompanying narrative, but you'll need to be close by to fill in the gaps in his memory and correct any misunderstandings he has.

Begin by asking your child what the first thing is that happened to him in his life. The obvious answer is that he was born, but if he's adopted, he very well may reply, "I came to live with you." In discussing his birth, talk about where he was born (city and state as well as specific location, such as a hospital) and the circumstances of his birth (who was there, what kind of birth it was, what time of day and day of the week).

An ideal time to discuss your child's birthparents is when you ask your child to draw a picture of his birthparents and write down what he knows about them. If you have more information or an actual photograph, this may be a good time to introduce it. Help correct any inaccuracies in your child's drawings or narratives by saying, for example, "You made your birthmother's hair brown, but I remember that it was red." Pay attention to the expressions on the birthparents' faces and ask your child why he thinks his birthmother was sad (or happy).

If you don't have information about your child's birthparents, ask him to draw what he thinks they look like and describe what he thinks they are like. Encourage your child to be realistic by correcting any fantasies, for example: "I know you would like to think that your birthfather was a Nobel Prize winner. He was probably an intelligent man, because you are intelligent, but probably not a famous man. How can you show that he's intelligent without making him a famous person?"

Continue to have your child record the significant events in his life, including his separation from his birthparent or birthparents and his entry into your family. Use the guidelines in this chapter for discussing unpleasant incidents such as abuse.

This is not the story of how your child joined your family, but the story of his life, so also include other significant events, such as starting school, achievements, a move to a new house, and the acquisition of a family pet.

You're obviously not going to be able to work through the first seven to eleven years of your child's life in one afternoon. Take your time. Evaluate when your child is beginning to get tired and suggest an end to the activity before it becomes frustrating. Remember that parts of his life story are going to evoke intense feelings for him. Give him a chance to express those feelings, and be available to talk about them. This may not follow immediately upon completion of the activity. Your child may mull over what he's written for the rest of the day and want to talk about it at bedtime. Keep that in mind and be open for any subtle signs that he wants to talk more about it. You might even introduce the topic later yourself:

Parent: "I've been thinking about your saying that your birthmother was sad when you were born because you are a boy. What did you mean?"

Be sure to ask your child what the "rules" are for sharing his lifebook. Is it something you can show other members of the family or discuss with his teacher?

You may find that your child is reluctant to make a lifebook. First, find out whether you're asking him to give up something more interesting to work on the lifebook, and if so, try to pick a more suitable time. If he still seems reluctant, consider that he may resist the idea because he senses it will be a painful experience, but don't necessarily give up the idea. If the lifebook is presented to your child as an opportunity for the two of you to share some special time, he is going to be more receptive to the idea. After all, most children this age still highly value their parents' undivided attention. You can also suggest the lifebook as something you need.

Parent: "I know you may not be very interested now, but I want to have a copy of your life story, written by you."

I think it's worth insisting that children make a lifebook. It helps them gather and sort through information about their origins, and it's a way for them to visually express their feelings about being adopted. But you have to evaluate the situation based on what you know about your child and what it means when he's being resistant to an idea.

A similar activity for parents and children who have been adopted is found in the workbook *Filling in the Blanks: A Guided Look at Growing Up Adopted,* by Susan Gabel (Available from Perspectives Press, P.O. Box 90318, Indianapolis, Ind. 46290-0318). Aimed at children ten years old and older, this workbook explains issues in adoption and asks children to record answers to specific questions dealing with their experiences and their reactions to those experiences.

Here I Am! A Lifebook Kit for Use with Children with Developmental Disabilities, by Susan Schroen (available from the National Resource Center for Special Needs Adoptions, P.O. Box 337, Chelsea, Mich. 48118), contains a workbook for children and a resource manual that parents can use.

5. "What Does Being Adopted Say About Me?"

The Middle Childhood Years

While watching the Olympics, my daughter expressed particular delight at seeing Olympic diver and adoptee Greg Louganis win a gold medal. A competitive swimmer herself, she said his win showed that people who were adopted could be good divers and swimmers. "Do you think people are surprised to find that out?" I asked. "Yes," she replied. "People think if you're different you're not as good."

Children in these middle years are gaining enough experience in the world to see themselves as distinct individuals. They compare their material possessions and their parents' occupations with those of their peers to determine their social status. They are more aware of their nationality or ethnic background and how that sets them apart from others. Children this age grapple to understand what differences mean outside the family. Is it good to be smart? Is it bad to be fat? Will being a strong basketball player make you more popular? Can girls do everything boys can do?

Around the age of seven, as children learn there is more than one kind of family, they become interested in their own family and with their place in their family.

For children who are adopted, these interests can lead to

questions such as: "What makes us a family?" "What does it mean to be the only adopted child in this family?" "What does it mean to be Asian–American in a Euro–American family and in a mostly Euro–American school and community?" and "Do people think adopted children are not as good as other people?"

In Chapter 4 we discussed how part of the struggle a child in the middle years has in making sense of adoption is intensely personal – the child wants to know why she was adopted when most children are not. The other part of the struggle is to understand the significance of being adopted in the family and in the world. Parents can help children explore these issues and express their feelings about being adopted in a world in which adoption is not the norm.

The child in the family

A parent once asked me, "How can I explain that adoption is as acceptable as having a baby when it was our second choice?"

Most parents do not think of adopting first when they start their families. Many choose adoption as a result of infertility. Others adopt after completing their biologic families, marrying someone with children, or deciding not to wait until they find a partner with whom they could have children.

Many people assume that because adoption was not our first choice, we have "settled" for less than we really wanted. Most of us discover, however, that raising children who are adopted meets or exceeds our original ideas of what being a parent would be like. We find out that while adoption may have been our second choice, it was not a second-best way of forming a family. However, whether adoption is second-best is one of the questions children in the middle childhood years have.

I like to tell people who think second choice is second-best about my hope when I was seventeen years old that I would be asked to the junior prom by a particular boy. He asked some-one else, and I went to the junior prom with my second choice. Four years later, we were married. Sometimes our second choice is the best choice for us.

Understanding why parents adopt

Children sometimes get a message from those outside the family that they should feel "grateful" to their parents for adopting them. Children must know that their parents had needs that were fulfilled by their adoption—adoptees don't have to behave a certain way or fulfill certain expectations to justify being in their families.

During these middle years, and particularly by the age of ten, children develop an understanding of why their parents decided to adopt. They believe, quite accurately, that parents adopt because of infertility, a desire to nurture children, or a desire for a child of a particular age or sex. They are increasingly able to evaluate intentions and recognize the importance of motives in evaluating a situation.

Even though you probably have talked before about why you wanted to adopt, your reasons need to be repeated at this time because your child can now understand them more fully. Her increased interest in and understanding of reproduction enables her to understand infertility or the difficulty of conceiving a child of a particular sex. And she can understand that you had needs that were met by adoption.

Child: "Did you get to pick me out?"

Parent: "No. We sent an application to the adoption agency. I don't know how they decided that you should come to live with us. Probably they had a list of children who needed to be adopted, and a list of parents who wanted to adopt children, and they just put each child with a set of parents."

Child: "Did you ask for a girl?"

Parent: "No. We said we didn't care if our child was a boy or a girl."

Child: "Could you have asked for a girl?"

Parent: "We could have, but it didn't matter to us. We could have asked for a boy with blue eyes and blonde hair whose birthparents were good at music and sports, if we'd wanted to. But all we wanted was a baby. So when they told us you would be our baby, we knew we had everything we wanted."

Children adopted through donor insemination, surrogacy, or *in vitro* fertilization also need to know why their parents chose the manner of conception they did:

Child: "Why didn't you just adopt a baby?"

Parent: "We wanted a baby who would grow inside mommy. Mommy and I wanted to be with you from the very moment you were conceived. We knew that even though we couldn't have a child who would come from me, we could still have a child who would come from mommy, and so we decided to try donor insemination."

Child: "Are you sorry you're not my real dad?"

Parent: "I was sad that I couldn't make a baby with mommy. But if mommy and I had made a baby together, that baby wouldn't be you. And I wouldn't trade you for anybody else in the world."

Despite having the intellectual ability to understand motives, children around the age of eleven typically become more critical of their parents and their parents' child-rearing practices. The desire of children to be part of the adult world, to have relationships outside the family, and to be an independent person leads them to confrontations with their parents. This is the age at which a child is likely to say something like, "I don't have to listen to you, you're not my real mother." Usually such statements attempt to distract parents from the real conflict they are having with their child, or are attempts to challenge parental authority. They may also be simply attention-getting statements, as the eleven-year-old desperately wants to be noticed. The astute parent will not allow himself to get drawn in to a discussion of reproduction or family formation at this point, but will direct the conversation back to the main point:

> Child: "You adopted me because you wanted a slave!"
>
> Parent: "We're not talking about how you joined our family. We're talking about doing your chores before you're allowed to go out with your friends. Right now, you are to do your chores. When we've both settled down, we can discuss whether your chores are too hard or whether you have too many. Get busy."

Relationship with siblings

Each child in a family has a unique story about how he or she joined that family. One may have been adopted traditionally, while another might have been adopted through donor insemination. One child may have been adopted through an open arrangement with the birthparents, while another may have little information about her birthparents. Parents sometimes wonder whether one child will feel jealous of the other because the other has more information about her birthparents, more involvement with them, or has joined the family in a way that seems more desirable. If they are normal children, there will be sibling rivalry, and they may use information about each other's entry into the family as ammunition during conflicts.

I was amused to see a television talk show host interview an adoptive mother about this very issue. She proudly proclaimed that her children, one adopted and one biologic, never taunted each other with statements such as "Mom chose me, but she had to take you." The talk show host turned to her teenage son, sitting beside her. "Is she right?" "Naw," he replied. "We used that stuff all the time."

Any time there are differences between children in a family, children may try to determine if being one way is better than being another. Often the more different the child is, the more she will think it's better to be the other way. To a great extent, parents have to let children work this out on their own. (See "When children tease," later in this chapter.) We cannot intervene in every squabble or try to make everything "equal" for our children. We must teach the difficult idea that being "fair" is not the same as being "equal," and that we can't even guarantee "fair."

We can't compensate for the inequalities or even the unfairness that may exist within our family. It wouldn't be right, for example, to ask one child's birthparent not to send gifts because your other children don't have that kind of relationship with their birthparents. Like other interactions in the family in which one child tries to "one-up" another, the best we can do is recognize that such interactions are likely to go on in the family, and let the hurt child know that we understand and are available for comfort.

Of course, sometimes a child is hurt because the difference between her and a sibling is important. For example, a child who has no contact with her birth family may feel hurt or angry when a sibling has contact with a birth relative because it may bring up feelings of rejection.

Therapist James Mahoney suggests that parents help their child express feelings at times like these by paraphrasing the child's statements.

Child: "Kevin's dad is stupid."

Parents: "It sounds like you don't like Kevin's birthfather."

Child: "Well, he writes Kevin these stupid letters and tells him how much he cares about him. If he really cared about him, he would've kept him."

Parent: "So you think that birthfathers who care about their children keep them."

Child: "Yeah. At least my birthfather isn't two-faced. He didn't care about me, so he didn't keep me, and he doesn't write me all the time to tell me something that isn't true."

Parent: "It sounds like you have some pretty strong feelings about your birthfather not writing to you."

Child: "Kevin always acts like it's such a big deal that his dad writes to him. I'd just like to get a letter so Kevin doesn't think he's so great."

Parent: "So you'd like to get a letter from your birthfather so that Kevin isn't the only one who hears from his birthfather."

Child: "Yeah. Why doesn't he ever write to me?"

Parent: "I don't know. But it sounds like you are sad and angry that he doesn't."

Child: "Sometimes."

Knowing that siblings are likely to compare and evaluate each other can help parents explain in a consistent way how each joined the family. For example, it isn't going to be sufficient to tell a child, "Your birthmother couldn't raise a baby because she was young and wasn't married," if the birthmother of another child in the family was married and in her thirties. The parent will have to go beyond the superficial explanation of the adoption plan to explain that birthmothers place their children for adoption because they feel unable to take on the responsibilities of parenthood at that time. Parents can explain that often it is harder for people to take on those responsibilities when they are very young and single, but that even mature, married women sometimes feel overwhelmed by the prospect of raising a baby.

When you explain the different ways that your children joined your family, make it clear you are happy with each situation. Don't try to minimize one child's experience because another child is feeling envious of it. If you can, think of a comparable situation that your child has experienced.

Parent: "Mommy and daddy wanted a baby very much and tried for a long time to make one, but we didn't. So we decided to adopt you, and we were very happy. Then I found out I was pregnant with Sam, and I was happy about that, too."

Child: "You love Sam more because he's really yours."

Parent: "Sam is biologically related to your father and to me, and we were very happy when he was born. But we are very happy to have you, too. You came into our family at a time when we really wanted a baby. We didn't want to have one more Christmas without a baby, and you arrived just in time so that we wouldn't have to. I love Sam because he's Sam, and I love you because you're you, and not having either one of you would be the worst thing in the world to me."

Child: "I still think you like Sam better."

Parent: "Do you remember when you got that stamp from Brazil for your stamp collection? You waited and waited and saved your money for a long time to be able to buy it. And you were so happy to have it because you had worked so hard for it and waited so long for it. And do you remember when your Aunt Debbie sent you a stamp from Malaysia? That didn't cost you anything and was a complete surprise, but you were happy to have it, too, because your aunt thought about you when she was on her trip and because nobody else at school has one like it. You like each one for itself."

One consistent source of jealousy, adoptive parents tell me, is that children who are adopted often get to celebrate "homecoming day" in addition to their birthdays. The children who were born into the family often think that is unfair. But it is also unfair to deny the family an opportunity to celebrate an important anniversary just because not every child in the family has a homecoming day.

In our family, we celebrate each child's homecoming day as a family anniversary rather than an individual one. Rather than receiving presents, the child whose homecoming day we are observing gets to select an activity that the entire family can participate in, such as going out to dinner, going to a movie, or going for a swim. The emphasis is on our family celebrating the child's arrival, rather than on the child celebrating joining a family.

The adopted child in the world

Just as children need to determine whether their parents consider it second-best to have adopted them, they need to explore how the rest of the world views adoption. As adults, we know that adoption is often misunderstood – we experienced the misunderstanding when we made plans to adopt. While we can't change that attitude overnight or shield our children from it, we can use our own experience to empathize with our child.

When children tease

One of the ways children assess the significance of differences is by teasing. They make fun of someone because of a particular difference and wait to see the person's reaction. If the taunt gets no response, the child concludes that characteristic is not an important one. But if the child being teased reacts by crying, getting angry, or running to an adult for comfort or intervention, the teaser may decide he has hit on something the other child is ashamed of.

Teasing is common among children in the primary grades. But it doesn't help parents or children to know that teasing is not only normal but an important part of child development. It still hurts to be teased. And it still hurts parents to see that their children are hurt.

Even though you can expect your child to be teased (and do some teasing of her own) when she enters school, and can probably predict what she'll be teased about, there's really no way to prepare your child for teasing without making her unnecessarily defensive. You can only hope that the efforts you have made so far to build positive self-esteem in your child and enable her to handle conflicts will carry her through these unpleasant experiences. You can also hope that you have been a model for your child when responding to adults who have made inappropriate remarks about the differences in your family.

Should your child share her experiences with you – and most school-age children will – resist your urge to minimize your child's pain by explaining away the other child's behavior ("Oh, I'm sure he didn't mean to hurt your feelings") or pointing out that everyone has differences. Also resist your urge to explode with outrage. Deal with your child's feelings – not your own.

I ask my children the following questions when they report hurtful incidents:

"What happened?"

This gives the child a chance to describe the incident.

"How did that make you feel?"

This gives the child a chance to express her feelings, which she may not have done at the time of the incident because she didn't want to let the other child know how hurt she was.

"What did you say or do when that happened?"

This gives the child an opportunity to think about how she responded, and lets her know that her parents think she is capable of handling such incidents herself.

"Are you happy with what you said (or did) or do you wish you had said (or done) something different?"

This is an important question because it allows the child to evaluate whether her response to the situation was appropriate and prepare for how she might handle the situation if it arises again. It also gives her a chance to express some angry feelings in a safe place. One little boy told his mother, "Next time I'm going to tell him that if he were in India, he's the one who would look funny!" If the child isn't sure how she could have responded differently, the parent can make suggestions, such as, "What do you think would have happened if you had said, 'Yeah, I'm adopted – so what'?"

"Is there anything you would like me to do?"

This lets your child know that her parents are available to help her if she wants help. Most children will not want their parents to get involved with playground conflicts, so if your child wants you to call the other child's parents, that could be a sign that the teasing is quite serious. If your child wants you to do something you are reluctant or unwilling to do, you can take the opportunity to talk about appropriate responses to the situation. For example, if a child says, "Make him stop," the parent will have to discuss whether that's within the realm of possibilities and what alternatives are available.

Part of the "value" of being teased is learning what it is appropriate to say to another person and learning how to handle upsetting remarks. If parents intervene whenever their child is teased, the child won't develop competence or confidence in handling difficult situations. Nevertheless, if the teasing progresses to bullying or seems to be damaging the child's self-esteem, parents might be justified in calling the other child's parents or school personnel – even if the child being teased doesn't want such intervention. While it's unlikely that such action will immediately change the bully's behavior, it may at least call attention to the problem.

Parents of minority children who attend schools with primarily Euro–American students might want to discreetly alert school personnel if their child is experiencing racist remarks. If the percentage of minority children is low, teachers and administrators might not be giving adequate attention to dealing with racism.

Another way to help your child deal with teasing is to share with her some of the remarks you have encountered because your family is different. In doing so, you're telling your child that just as she sometimes feels different because of her race or status in the family, sometimes your whole family feels different because of the way it was formed or its ethnic make-up. Choose your incident carefully – you don't want one that is going to again point to your child's differences or make her feel responsible for people being rude to you. Select one in which the person making the remark is made to appear foolish.

One father, whose child was being teased because he is African–American, told his child of the time when they encountered a stranger who looked at the African–American child, then looked at the Euro–American father, then looked at the African–American child again and remarked, "He must look like his mother." The father replied, "Yes, he does." The child, who was old enough to understand, laughed uproariously at the joke played on the stranger.

Racial and ethnic awareness

By the time children enter school they understand that people can be grouped according to their physical characteristics, that these groups have different social status, and to which of these groups they belong (see "Racial awareness and attitudes" in Chapter 3). As they enter school, unsure of their place in the world, children try to determine – often by teasing – whether racial or ethnic differences make an individual inferior.

The minority child

In Chapter 2 we discussed how parents must help their

children learn about their racial or ethnic heritage so they can be proud of their cultural roots, and prepare their children for the discrimination they will encounter as members of a minority group. The importance of this becomes more apparent during the middle childhood years.

One parent was delighted that her second-grade daughter had enough pride in her ethnic origins to make a presentation to her class about Korea. The project went well, but a few weeks later, the daughter came home in tears because children on the playground had been taunting her about her "flat face."

It isn't surprising that transracially adopted children are often knowledgeable about their cultural origins and proud of them, but unprepared for what it feels like to be a member of a minority group. Judging from the comments of parents who adopt transracially, most make an effort to acquaint their children with their heritage through dolls and other toys, folk tales and picture books, television programs, cookbooks, cassette tapes, and the myriad of other items available. But they are often unaware that this isn't enough to prepare the child for racial discrimination and prejudice.

Because everyone is a member of some ethnic group, it may be easy for parents to recognize the importance of cultural awareness and know how to meet that need for their children. But because being Euro–American is "okay," parents who are not members of minority groups themselves may not understand the implications or importance of race to those who are.

It's even more important than it was when their children were younger for parents to expand the family's cultural exploration beyond their children's ethnic or racial group to those of other minorities. Children need to see that minority groups have made important contributions to the world in music, art, architecture, dance, science, mathematics, boat-building, agriculture, and other disciplines.

Children also need heroes and role models who are

members of minority groups so that they know that Asian–Americans, African–Americans, East Indian–Americans, Jewish–Americans, and others are recognized for their accomplishments. When members of minority groups see that someone in any minority group is "making it," it tells them, "Minorities are not inferior," and "Being part of a minority does not have to hold you back."

One family started a scrapbook of people who would make good role models. The parents make an effort to include individuals other than Euro–American males, including women, disabled individuals, and members of minorities. The role models include athletes, politicians, artists, scientists, and members of the local community.

Experiencing being in the majority

It's valuable for children to experience being in the majority – even if it is only occasionally. While racially integrated communities and schools are valuable for transracially adopted children, the minority children are often still in the minority.

Culture camp is one way for children to experience being in the majority. Some adoption agencies and organizations, particularly those that deal with large numbers of children from Korea, offer such week-long experiences for children eight and older during the summer. The primary purpose of these camps is to acquaint children with the culture of their heritage through songs, games, foods, and other activities. But the real benefit is probably the opportunity for children to be with others who share their heritage and their adoptive status.

Some families consider a trip to their child's country of birth during these middle childhood years. But some people who have led such trips have told me it is difficult for young children to sustain interest in tourist activities. Young children sometimes have difficulty adapting to aspects of a foreign country, such as different toilets, different foods, and different climate. They recommend that adoptees wait until about the age of twenty-one before returning to their country of birth.

Others, however, say that children ten to twelve years old are at an ideal age for a trip to their homeland. They are mature enough for foreign travel, yet still young enough to enjoy being with their parents.

Parents who decide to visit their child's country of birth should take the time to prepare their child not only for a foreign lifestyle, but for the emotions that are likely to be unleashed, and prepare themselves for dealing with those emotions.

Parent: "What do you think it will be like to go back to the orphanage you were in?"

Child: "I don't think I'll remember anybody. And they won't remember me."

Parent: "Probably not. While we're there, I'm going to ask if we can look in your records to find out if there's any more information about your birthparents."

Child: "What will you do if you find out who they are?"

Parent: "What would you like me to do?"

Child: "I don't know."

Parent: "Would you like to try to find your birthparents if we can?"

Child: "Well, I probably wouldn't be able to talk to them because we don't speak the same language."

Parent: "That's true. Would you rather not see them if you can't talk to them?"

Child: "Well, no. I'd like to see them."

Parent: "Do you think they'd like to see you even though you couldn't talk to each other?"

Child: "Well, probably not."

Parent: "Why not?"

Child: "They've probably forgotten about me."

Parent: "I think they'd like to see what a neat kid you turned out to be. After all, they made you."

Child: "Yeah, maybe."

Parent: "How would you feel if we got there and couldn't find out any more about you and couldn't find anyone at the orphanage who remembers you?"

Child: "I don't know. I guess I'd be sad."

Parent: "I'd be sad, too. But I'd be glad we had tried."

When children reach adolescence, they may look to racial or ethnic clubs as a way to expand their racial awareness and experience being in the majority.

Racially ambiguous children

As we discussed in Chapter 3, parents of a child whose biologic parents were of two different races, or whose own race cannot be accurately determined by appearance, should not be concerned with what other people think or with what the child initially thinks is her race. Children classify themselves by race the same way other people classify them—by their appearance. Efforts to convince a preschooler that he is African–American when he has no African–American features will only confuse the child. And it is no one else's business. It is recommended, however, that parents expose the child to African–American culture because eventually she will be able to understand that she has an African–American heritage as well as a Euro–American heritage.

School-age children's interest in their birthparents will provide opportunities to discuss their racial heritage. In such discussions, avoid the terms "biracial" or "mixed race," which are meaningless in our society. Historically, Euro–Americans and Asians have demanded that individuals be "racially pure" to belong to their racial group. And historically, African–Americans and Hispanics have been racially mixed.

Child: "My birthmother was Hispanic, right?"

Parent: "Yes."

Child: "And my birthfather was African–American?"

Parent: "Yes."

Child: "What does that make me?"

Parent: "What do you think?"

Child: "People always ask me if I'm black."

Parent: "That's what some people say when they mean African–American."

Child: "I guess I do look more like my birthfather."

Parent: "It's not important for other people to know everything about your birthparents. But it is important for you to know that you have Hispanic ancestry as well as African–American."

Social worker Azizi Powell recommends telling children of mixed ancestry that many important people were of mixed ancestry. She also suggests that parents prepare their children for the possibility of being mislabeled as a result of their physical features. For example, the parents of a dark-skinned East Indian child could ask her what she would say if someone mistook her for an African–American.

If we have exposed our children to cultures other than their own, and have communicated by our actions that all minority groups are valuable, we can hope that a child will not feel embarrassed or stigmatized at being mistaken for a member of a minority group to which she does not belong.

Ethnic awareness and nationality

Whenever we talk with children about "nationality," we have to be clear about whether we are talking about citizenship or ethnic group—both acceptable meanings for "nationality." If this seems confusing, imagine how difficult it is for a child who has only a simple understanding of political boundaries, race, ethnic groups, citizenship, and biological connections.

Child: "I'm Filipino, right?"

Parent: "You're Filipino because you were born in the Philippines to Filipino birthparents. You're an American because you are a citizen of the United States. That means you have all the privileges of any other U.S. citizen, including the right to vote for our leaders. You can say you are a Filipino–American."

Child: "Where's Dean from?"

Parent: "Dean's from Missouri."

Child: "I thought he was from Africa."

Parent: "The United States is made up of people from all over the world. Some of them came here a long time ago from places like Africa, Europe, and China. They had children here and their children grew up and had children. They're citizens of the United States if they are born here. If their great-great-great-great grand-parents were from Africa, they probably have dark skin, but lots of people with dark skin are born in the United States. We call them African–Americans, although some people call them black.

"Some people move to the United States after being born in another country, like you, and become citizens of the United States. They may still feel like they belong to the country they were born in because they remember it and have friends and relatives who live there, but they may also feel that they belong to the United States because they have chosen this for their country."

Parents can use historical events, such as the internment of Japanese–Americans during World War II, to discuss how they would resolve a conflict between loyalty to ethnic group and loyalty to their country. While watching the Olympics, our family has had interesting conversations about athletes competing for countries of which they are citizens against athletes from their countries of origin.

Confusing race and nationality

The concept of race as distinctive of nationality can be even more difficult. Explaining to a child, for example, that she is both Korean and Asian–American is difficult until she can understand the concept of countries and peoples.

Child: "Is Mary Beth Korean?"

Parent: "No, she's Chinese–American."

Child: "But she looks just like Sarah, and Sarah's Korean."

Parent: "Mary Beth and Sarah are both Asian. That means that their ancestors all came from the same part of the world and had some of the same physical features. But Asia is made up of a lot of different countries, just as North America is made up of more than one country–Canada and the United States. Korea is a country in Asia, and so is China. Mary Beth's family came from China a long time ago, and Sarah's family still lives in Korea. Sarah is Asian–American because she was born in Korea and her birthparents are Korean. Mary Beth was born in the United States and so were her parents. But she's still Asian–American because she comes from an Asian family and shares their physical features. You don't have light skin just by being born in the United States. You have to be born to people with light skin."

Talking with school personnel

At her first parent–teacher conference, one parent mentioned to her child's teacher that she and the girl's father were divorced. "Oh," the teacher responded. "I hadn't noticed any problems."

Adoptive parents are often reluctant to share information

about their child's origins with school personnel. They want their child's teacher to have enough information about the child to understand his needs, yet they don't want their child's teacher to be looking for problems just because the child is from a nontraditional family. Unfortunately, we can't assume that teachers or school personnel will have any better attitudes toward children in nontraditional families than anyone else in society. As discussed in Chapter 1, society considers it a problem for a person to be different.

Working with school personnel

Because children in the middle childhood years are working through a lot of issues concerning how they joined their families, it is important for teachers to be aware of the child's adoption and the issues the child might have as a result.

Pediatrician Vera Fahlberg recommends that parents ask the teacher early in the school year whether the class will be working on any projects or having any activities involving family or personal origins. Once aware of any activities that could be distressing or difficult to the child because of her adoption, parents and teacher together can decide how the activity can be structured or simply be more alert to signs that the child is having difficulty.

Teachers are generally open to learning more about the special needs of their students. Your efforts at explaining the kinds of issues adopted children have are likely to be more successful if they are part of ongoing communication between you and the school, rather than as reactions to crises or problems. If you only discuss adoption when there is a problem, it may appear that you are using adoption as an excuse for your child's behavior or think your child deserves some kind of special treatment. You may also put the teacher on the defensive.

Parent–teacher conferences tend to be brief, so you won't be able to fully educate school personnel at those times. But you can explain some adoption issues and give the teacher a copy of a book or article that will expand on your discussion. One article for school personnel is "Adoption," by Candice A. Hughes, in *Children's Needs: Psychological Perspectives*, edited by Alex Thomas and Jeff Grimes (Washington, D.C.: The National Association of School Psychologists, 1987).

You can also volunteer to put together a workshop for all the teachers in the school or school district to acquaint them with the issues adopted children have. More parents are telling me that they are speaking to groups of teachers and school personnel about adoption issues – an encouraging trend. Make sure your children know you are not going to share anything with these groups that they would find embarrassing. And if they indicate they don't want you to speak to the teachers at their school, try educating the teachers at another school.

You may want to suggest that the school district adopt the curriculum project developed for social studies or home economics classes in which adoption is discussed in appropriate ways for elementary school and high school students. "Adoption Builds Families" (available from the Social Science Education Consortium, 855 Broadway, Boulder, Colo. 80302) has materials suitable for kindergarten through senior high school.

The teacher is unlikely to take offense or become defensive at your attempts to educate her if you do it in a way that says, "I know you will want to know about this because you are a sensitive, caring teacher who wants to meet the needs of all your students."

Sharing confidential information

While it's important for school personnel to have pertinent information about the children in their schools, parents can't assume that school personnel will understand the confidential nature of the information they are given, since even parents sometimes are confused about what is appropriate to share with those outside the family.

When you share information about your child's origins with teachers, let them know you are sharing the information with them as a professional and you expect the information to be held in professional confidence. Tell them you expect them to ask you or your child for permission before sharing the information with anyone else.

If you are sharing information that you have not yet told your child, make sure the teacher or counselor is aware of this. If your child is not aware that you are sharing information, the school should know this as well.

It is possible to give school personnel information they need without giving them all the details about the child's history. For example, if your child is acting out sexually, you can tell the schoolteacher that this is a problem, explain that your child is getting appropriate counseling, and let them know what you would like them to do *without* explaining that she was molested prior to her adoption. Explaining the history of the problem in that situation serves the interests of the adoptive parents more than the child.

Activity: Making a family tree

When your child reaches the fourth or fifth grade, she may be asked to make a family tree for a classroom assignment. How to complete the assignment is often a dilemma for the child, who doesn't know whether to depict her adoptive family or her birth family – or both. This dilemma can be compounded if she thinks her adoptive parents would be hurt if she drew a biologic family tree, or if she doesn't have much information about her biologic family to include in a family tree. But if she perceives that the purpose of the assignment is to depict one's ancestors, she may feel that she would be completing the assignment incorrectly by turning in a family tree of her adoptive family. It isn't unusual for a child to conclude that neither alternative is acceptable and simply fail to turn in the assignment.

Parents can help their children make family trees that depict their unique histories, and in doing so, tell their children that they believe both the adoptive and biologic histories are important.

While many adoptive parents shy away from genealogical activities, making a family tree is such a good opportunity for family discussion, including discussion about extended family members (see "Activity: Getting to know the extended family" in Chapter 3), that you may not want to wait for a school assignment. When you child is about nine, find a way to illustrate her dual heritage.

Birth Family

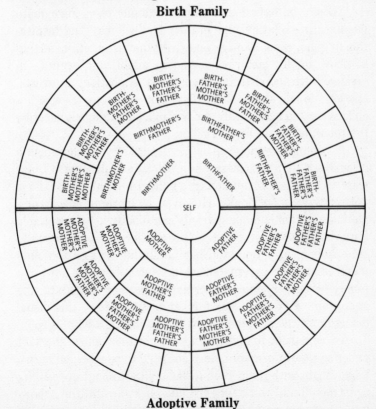

Adoptive Family

Figure 1. Half-wheel

The half-wheel

A half-wheel is often used by genealogists to show a pedigree – the individuals from whom one is descended. The difference between a pedigree and a family tree is that the pedigree does not show siblings. The child can fill in a half-wheel for the adoptive family and a half-wheel for the biologic family and join the two halves, with herself at the center. This not only graphically depicts the child's dual heritage, but shows that when both are depicted, the circle is complete.

Genograms

Those who have found standard family trees inadequate for depicting relationships in their families may find inspiration in genograms. Genograms go beyond listing descendants to show family histories, including significant events, individual characteristics, occupations, education, interests, and emotional relationships. They not only show to whom a child is related biologically and through adoption, but describe the relationships in both families.

A complete genogram is more suitable for therapeutic discussions than for classroom projects, and parents will not want to include information on a genogram that their child is not ready for emotionally. However, by learning how a complete genogram is made, parents can modify it to be suitable for a classroom project and can use a fuller version at home to help their child understand her family history. As the child matures and the parents share more details about her birth family with her, more information can be added to the genogram. As we discuss further in Chapter 6, this visual depiction of the adoptee's birth family can be advantageous.

To construct a genogram, start with a large sheet of paper so that information does not need to be crowded onto a page. Begin with the person for whom the genogram is being constructed and work forward and backward in time, showing marriages and separations, the birth and adoption of children, major illnesses and deaths.

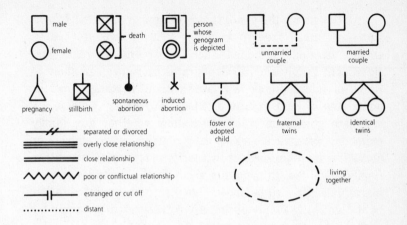

Figure 2. Key to genograms

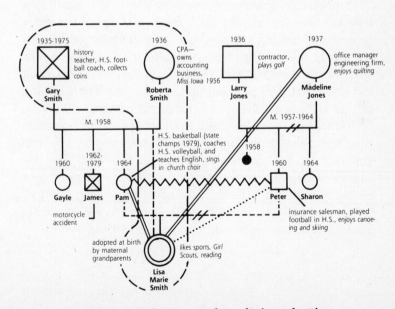

Figure 3. Genogram for relative adoption

At this point, the genogram is not much different from a standard family tree. It becomes fuller when information about individuals is added, such as careers, interests, and significant family events. Genograms therefore can show to whom an adopted child is related without needing names or birthdates of birth relatives, which may be unavailable. (A complete genogram would also show whether any family members were alcoholics or drug abusers, were abusive or abused, were depressed, or had serious arguments with other family members. Information about family attitudes toward individuals can also be shown, such as, "disappointed father by not entering family business," or "respected by family for work in the women's movement.")

An important part of the genogram is the depiction of the quality of relationships within the family. Lines can be drawn between family members to indicate whether they had a relationship that was close, overly close, distant, or characterized by conflict. Genograms can also show who in the family lives together. For the adopted child, this solves one of the major problems of making a family tree – how to visually show how her family relationships have been affected by adoption. The adoptee can show that she is biologically related to people but also show that their relationship has been cut off or is distant, or that she doesn't live with her biologic parents.

Genograms are also useful in showing how current situations may be influenced by family patterns going back several generations. For example, a genogram may show that the youngest daughter in each generation became pregnant as a teenager and placed the child for adoption. Seeing this pattern in her biologic family might help a child see her birthmother's situation from a different point of view.

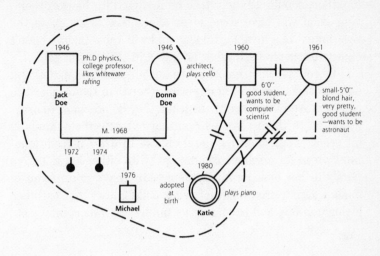

Figure 4. Genogram for traditional adoption

For more about genograms see: *Working With Adoptive Families Beyond Placement,* by Ann Hartman (New York: Child Welfare League of America, 1984); *Finding Families: An Ecological Approach to Family Assessment in Adoption,* by Ann Hartman (Beverly Hills: SAGE Publications, 1979); *Family Therapy in Clinical Practice,* by Murray Bowen (New York: Aronson, 1978); and *Genograms in Family Assessment,* by Monica McGoldrick and Randy Gerson (New York: W.W. Norton, 1985).

A final word

Not everyone agrees that a child's adoptive and biologic families should be depicted on the same family tree. What is important is that children be aware of options they have to visually depict their families.

After you've made a genogram or a half-wheel pedigree

together, should a family tree be assigned in the classroom, your child will have some ideas about how to complete the assignment in a meaningful way and will know that you don't object to her discussing her adoption in this way at school.

Of course, children often are uncomfortable completing a homework assignment in any way other than the teacher has outlined. And there are times when they do not want to draw attention to themselves by pointing out how their family is different. Your child may still choose to draw a traditional family tree for a school assignment (with either her adoptive family or her biologic family depicted). That's fine. If you've made a family tree together, your child knows that both her biologic family and her adoptive family are important.

6. "Who Am I?"
Adolescence

The teenager's task is developing an identity – discovering how he is different from every other human being who has ever lived, as well as how he is connected to the people he considers "his people."

Identity involves sexual self-image, intellectual capabilities, talents, beliefs, physical characteristics, racial and ethnic heritage, personality traits, interests, and relationships with peers and family. Not surprisingly, becoming aware of one's self as a unique individual involves becoming more independent, both physically and mentally.

Teens develop their sense of who they are by seeing how they are alike and different from those who are most like them – their families. They also perceive how others see them, which may involve expectations based on gender, physical appearance, family membership, or cultural heritage.

This task is difficult for any adolescent, but those with more than two parents find it even more complicated, especially if they don't know much about their biologic family. It is difficult for a person to have a sense of being physically unique when he is wondering whether there are biologic relatives who look like him. It is difficult for a person to feel connected to the history of a people when he doesn't know his ethnic background. It is difficult for him to feel independent of his parents when he has parents he has never met. It is difficult for a member of a minority to feel part of a racial or ethnic culture when he is raised in a family with a different heritage. It may be difficult to nurture musical ability in a family that doesn't appreciate music. It is difficult to live up to expectations others have that are based on a family relationship that does not exist, for example, that a child in the family will be as intelligent as his parents.

Even teenagers who have contact with their biologic parents have a more complicated task in identity formation because they have two sets of parents to whom they must compare themselves.

Teenagers usually aren't aware they're trying to establish an identity. They explore identity issues out of a need to feel emotionally at peace. They're able to explore identity issues because they have achieved a new stage in mental development – abstract thinking.

Unlike younger children who can only think in concrete terms, adolescents can think about thinking itself. This enables them to consider more than one viewpoint at a time, viewpoints other than their own, and viewpoints contrary-to-fact, and follow them to their logical conclusions. This ability enables adolescents to engage in scientific and philosophical thinking.

Psychologists believe that abstract thinking begins to develop in most teenagers around the ages of eleven or twelve. It takes several years of using these new skills – typically until age fifteen or sixteen – before the adolescent can use them comfortably. In the meantime, adolescents often become confused, self-conscious, withdrawn, confrontational, and otherwise hard to live with.

Parents can help adolescents in their search for identity by understanding their need for factual information about themselves, including their origins; by allowing them the freedom to explore identity issues, such as religious values and ethnic identity; and by helping them refine the mental abilities necessary for that exploration.

Developing a factual basis for identity

While it might be sufficient to talk with younger children about what their birthparents "probably" were like or what their situation "probably" was, adolescents need more definite information. Teenagers may have difficulty thinking of the birthparents as real individuals if they have little or no specific information about them. Those adopted through donor insemination or *in vitro* fertilization with a donor egg or donor embryo may have a particularly hard time believing they are descended from real human beings.

At the same time, adolescents need to think about their birthparents realistically because they can imagine many possible situations and need help sorting through them. Providing them with concrete evidence is a good way to do that.

For this reason, with rare exceptions, adolescents should have all the available information about their origins. Otherwise, their new ability to hypothesize—to take an idea and follow it through to its logical conclusions—may lead them to some incorrect and worrisome ideas about their birthparents and their adoption. For example, some minor physical ailment might lead them to believe they have an incurable inherited disease. Or they might decide that their birthmother was a prostitute, or their birthfather was a rapist.

To the adolescent, who is plagued with worries about everything from whether his skin will ever be clear to whether nuclear war will break out, knowing the truth about his origins—even if it involves some unpleasant information—is better than imagining all the possibilities.

Providing the final details

I often hear adoptive parents express their justifiable

outrage when they discover that information about their child's history was withheld from them. They say they can handle anything in the child's past, but they need all the available information if they are to make sense of what is going on with a child.

If that's how we feel as parents, imagine how adoptees feel. They, too, need all the available information about themselves to make sense of who they are. They, too, opt for information and truth over wondering and confusion, even if the truth involves some pain.

If you have been providing your child with information about his origins with the intent of adding details as his ability to understand them increases (see "Explaining difficult situations" in Chapter 4), it may still be difficult to provide final details, particularly if the teenager's birthparents were involved in activities such as prostitution, drug use, incest, or physical abuse. With a little planning, however, it is possible to explain what happened in a way that does not condone their actions, but allows the teenager to view the situation in a way that will leave him feeling all right about being related to that person.

The abstract thinking of teenagers enables them to see things from others' viewpoints. Adolescents are also more likely to judge an individual's actions by his motives or intentions rather than by the consequences. Parents can use the teenager's ability to see alternatives to help him realize that he has choices other than those his birthparents made.

Parent: "You know that your birthmother was very young when you were born. She was only sixteen. One of the other things we know about her is that she ran away from home when she was fourteen."

Teen: "Why did she do that?"

Parent: "She had some serious problems in her family. Her stepfather was sexually abusing her."

Teen: "You mean he was having sex with her?"

Parent: "Yes, and she apparently didn't know how to stop it except to run away."

Teen: "That's not what I would do."

Parent: "What would you do?"

Teen: "Well, I would call the police or tell my counselor at school."

Parent: "I think those are good choices. Why do you think they would be better than running away?"

Teen: "Because then he'd get punished. If I ran away, he might just start doing it to somebody else."

Parent: "And why would running away not be good for you?"

Teen: "Well, if you went to a friend's house or to your grandmother's house, they'd just tell your parents, and you'd probably have to go back and it would just start all over again."

Parent: "What if you went somewhere where they couldn't find you?"

Teen: "Then you wouldn't have any money or any way to live."

Parent: "That's what happened to your birthmother. She went to a place where she didn't know anybody and didn't have any way to get money. She was only fourteen. Nobody was going to hire her for a real job."

Teen: "So what did she do?"

Parent: "She found a man who said he'd take care of her if she'd work for him. Only the job he had for her was prostitution."

Teen: "I'd never do that—even if I was starving to death."

Parent: "You probably have too much respect for yourself. And I'm glad that you do. But sometimes, when you are young and someone keeps forcing you to have sex with them, the way your birthmother's stepfather did, you get used to people using you for their pleasure and you begin to think that's all you're good for."

Sexual abuse, rape, incest, physical abuse, and other unpleasant topics can be explained in similar ways.

For example, parents can explain rape as an act of violence. They can say that the birthfather who raped knew that rape was an unacceptable way to behave (demonstrated by his telling the victim he'd kill her if she told anyone about the rape), but had not learned nonviolent ways of expressing anger.

Teenagers imagine that people are scrutinizing them closely. They have a tendency to believe people know their most private thoughts. When you discuss unpleasant information about his origins with your teenager, be sure to reassure him that the information is private.

Parent: "What we've told you today is something that only the social worker, mom and dad know – and now you. The social worker is bound to keep such information confidential. We haven't told any relatives – even grandma and grandpa. We haven't told your teachers. We haven't told anyone else. We kept the information to ourselves not because we are ashamed of it – you weren't responsible for what happened – but because we felt it should be your decision to share this information with other people when you were old enough."

Using genograms in adolescence

A genogram (described in the Activity section of Chapter 5) is a useful way to graphically depict what is known about an individual's family history. It enables an adolescent who is adopted to see the interests, talents, personality traits, occupations, and achievements of his birth family as well as his adoptive family, which is important in his identity formation.

When there is negative information, such as a family history of alcholism or abuse, a genogram can show how these problems may have been influenced by behavior patterns in the family or stressful family circumstances.

Author and social work educator Ann Hartman suggests that genograms also enable adoptees to see that even though their birthparents may have had serious problems, other members of their biologic families have been mentally, physically, and emotionally healthy.

Idealizing the birthparents

Teenagers who lack information about their birthparents may idealize them. Abstract thinking enables teenagers to set up ideals because they can consider ideas that are contrary-to-fact and follow them through to their logical conclusions. They can imagine their parents as perfect, their boyfriends or girlfriends as perfect, their families as perfect, and themselves as perfect. But unlike younger children who ignore evidence that doesn't support the conclusion they want, teenagers measure reality against their ideals, inevitably concluding that their lives and the people in them are inadequate.

Adolescents who are frustrated at the imperfections in their own parents naturally fantasize about having other parents. And the teenager who actually has other parents is no exception. Like the child of divorce, who believes his life would be completely different (and infinitely better) if he lived with his noncustodial parent, the adolescent who has been adopted may believe his birthparents would wear more acceptable clothing, listen to better music, and be more understanding than his adoptive parents. He may even fantasize that his birthparents are the movie stars or rock stars he so idolizes.

In many cases, the teenager's birthparents are much younger than the adoptive parents, adding to the fantasy that the birthparents would be much more understanding and acceptable. The birthparents may also be a more romantic couple, seen through the eyes of the adolescent as forever caught up in the passion that resulted in his own conception, compared to the adoptive parents who are seen in the day-to-day reality of a mature relationship. This is particularly true if the infertility of his adoptive parents has caused the teenager to question their sexuality. The adolescent may conclude the birthparents would be better able to relate to his own passionate feelings.

Acknowledge your teenager's desire for life to be the way he would like it to be, but encourage him to test his ideals against reality:

Parent: "Would you please turn down your stereo."

Teen: "You are so old-fashioned!"

Parent: "What do you mean?"

Teen: "Well, you hate my music. You hate the way I wear my hair. You hate my clothes. You want me to look like a freak and listen to the Beatles! You guys are just so old you can't remember how it feels to be young!"

Parent: "Do you think any parent remembers what it feels like to be young?"

Teen: "It's probably a lot easier if you're thirty than if you're fifty!"

At this point, parents might wonder whether the teenager is thinking about his birthparents, but be reluctant to explore that idea for fear of bringing adoption into a discussion in which it really doesn't belong. Parents have to trust their instincts in a situation like this, exploring adoption issues if they seem relevant, and dropping them if they don't. For example:

Parent: "Your birthparents are about thirty. Do you

think they would enjoy the same kind of music you do and like the way you wear your hair?"

Teen: "I dunno. Maybe."

Parent: "It's an interesting question. Maybe you could write to them and find out."

Nothing has really been settled here, but you've reminded your teenager that there are different ways of looking at the same situation. You've let him know you're not concerned that he might be comparing you to his birthparents, but you've reminded him that if he is fantasizing about his birthparents, there may be evidence that contradicts his ideas.

When information is lacking

If you have an open adoption, in which you and the birthparents have made a commitment to stay in touch with each other, obtaining information will be much easier than in a situation in which confidentiality was promised.

If you don't have a lot of details about the birthparents, it isn't too late to obtain them, although it's certainly easier to seek information when the child is younger and the need for information seems less urgent. Some parents contact the agency, doctor, or intermediary used in the adoption with requests for more information. Others believe it is the teenager's responsibility to seek more information, but support their teenagers' efforts. Individual families will need to work out the arrangement that seems best for them.

Even if no information is uncovered, it can be important to the parent–teen relationship for the teen to know that his parents understand his need for information. So some parents document their efforts to discover more details about their children's origins, for example, by keeping copies of any letters of inquiry – even though they may have learned nothing as a result of their efforts.

If finding out more information about the birthparents is impossible, as it would be with many adoptions, this doesn't necessarily mean your teenager's development will be stunted. There are many things teenagers worry about yet can't resolve other than by accepting the situation. Some are able to put their adoption experience in perspective without additional information, while others find the lack of information a constant source of uncertainty.

Therapist Claudia Jewett suggests that whenever teenagers are concerned about events beyond their control – whether it is a lack of information about birthparents or famine in Africa – that parents help them look at the situation realistically.

Parent: "What bothers you the most about not being able to find out anything about your birthparents?"

Teen: "Well, they might have some bad disease that I could get."

Parent: "That's a legitimate concern. Do you worry about a particular disease?"

Teen: "Mostly I worry that one of them might be crazy and I'll be crazy, too."

Parent: "What if you got a letter today saying your birthfather was schizophrenic? What could you do about that?"

Teen: "What's schizophrenic?"

Parent: "Schizophrenia is a disorder of thoughts and feelings. If you knew your birthfather had schizophrenia, what could you do about that?"

Teen: "Nothing. I'm not a psychiatrist."

Parent: "How would knowing that he was schizophrenic change your life right now?"

Teen: "If I started feeling crazy or something, like I started thinking about killing myself, then I'd know I probably was crazy."

Parent: "Are you feeling crazy or thinking about suicide?"

Teen: "No."

Parent: "I'm glad to hear that. You don't seem mentally ill to me, either. If you did start feeling crazy or thinking about suicide would you try to get help even if you didn't know anything about your birthfather?"

Teen: "Well, if I was going crazy I might not know I was acting crazy."

Parent: "Those around you who care about you would probably see that you weren't behaving normally and would try to help you, even though they wouldn't know your family history."

Teen: "Well, I'd still like to know."

Parent: "I can understand that."

It may seem to you or to your teenager that the only way to answer the questions he has about his origins is to meet his birthparents. In Chapter 7, we examine the advantages and disadvantages of contact with birthparents during adolescence.

Building a physical identity

Like other teenagers, adopted adolescents are concerned about their physical appearance. But in addition to the usual anxieties they have as a result of their developing bodies, teenagers who are adopted wonder whether they look like anyone else. And they may be uncomfortable with their bodies as a result of physical differences between them and their parents or siblings.

Adolescents' preoccupation with appearance is brought on in part by the rapid changes in physical appearance during puberty. But there is more to it than that. Abstract thinking enables them to understand that other people could be thinking about them. This makes them feel continually on display and contributes to their intense desire for privacy.

If you've forgotten what this is like, perhaps you can remember what it was like to attend your high school reunion.

Back among the people you knew as adolescents, you may have begun to relate to them as you did as an adolescent, believing people were watching you more closely than they were. You may have tried to lose ten pounds before the reunion, or imagined what people would think when they saw your spouse. Imagine feeling like that day after day and you have recaptured what it feels like to be a teenager.

Furthermore, adolescents' propensity to set up ideals is not limited to others. They can imagine themselves as physically perfect, but recognize they aren't. Their belief that everyone is looking at them only adds to their disgust at their imperfections. Not only are they imperfect, but everyone can see it.

The face in the mirror

Adopted teenagers' preoccupation with their appearance may cause them to speculate about whether they look like anyone. They also want to know what their birth relatives look like as a way of determining how unique they are physically, and as a way of feeling connected to past generations. (See "Developing a family identity," later in this chapter.)

One mother was stunned when she looked at her son's most recent school picture. A physical maturity was clearly evident in his face that she had not noticed before. As she began to look at him becoming an adult, she realized he looked like someone and could understand his curiosity about his birthparents when he looked in the mirror.

One of the benefits of open adoptions is that they provide families with opportunities for obtaining photographs of the birth relatives or having personal contact with them.

If you already have photographs of your adolescent's birthparents that you have not shared with him, do so now. Don't wait for him to ask for them, even if he knows you have them. He may have forgotten about them, may think it would hurt your feelings to ask for them, or may not want you to know he's interested in his birthparents. You can also initiate conversations about his birthparents' appearance:

> Parent: "Look at the picture we got of your cousin Elizabeth. Doesn't she look a lot like your Uncle Chris? Sometimes I look in the mirror and I think I'm looking at a picture of my mother thirty-five years ago. Do you ever wonder if you look like your birthparents?"

Teenagers are pretty astute, so you won't be able to set up a situation like this. It must be an honest expression of your feelings. What you can do, however, is be open to your own feelings so that when an opportunity presents itself, you are ready to use it.

Too many faces

Because a single biologic father in donor insemination may father dozens (and potentially hundreds) of children, those adopted through donor insemination often wonder if they are seeing a half-sibling whenever they encounter someone who resembles them.

One man told me he once had a stranger insist that they had been together at a party the previous evening. On another occasion, his close friend of many years was convinced that the two of them had been talking together for more than ten minutes, and wondered why there seemed to be no recognition. In fact, the two were hundreds of miles apart. This man is so struck by the resemblance between himself and a member of his local symphony orchestra that he frequently walks past the musician's house and attends symphony functions, hoping to develop a relationship that will enable him to ask the intensely personal question: "Were you adopted through donor insemination, too?"

To dismiss such encounters as coincidence is to miss the point: Adoptees wonder if they look like any of their birth relatives and if anyone they look like might be a birth relative.

If you notice your teenager staring at someone with similar physical features, give him an opportunity to explore his concerns:

Parent: "You seem to be staring at that man. He does kind of look like you, doesn't he?"

Teen: "Yeah, I guess so."

Parent: "Does that make you wonder if you two are related?"

Teen: "Sort of."

Parent: "How old do you think he is?"

Teen: "I don't know. About twenty-two maybe."

Parent: "You're fifteen. Probably not your birthfather."

Teen: "Not unless he was a very mature little boy."

Parent: "Right. How about a brother or half-brother?"

Teen: "Could be."

Parent: "Shall we ask him?"

Teen: "Right. 'Excuse me, but are we brothers?' "

Parent: "You were born a thousand miles from here. What do you think the chances are that you and a birth brother would both be in this town, at this restaurant, at the same time?"

Teen: "Well, maybe he moved here, too."

Parent: "It's possible. If you found out he was your brother, what would you do?"

Teen: "Tell him to wear a different tie with that shirt."

Parent: "Good point. But you know what I mean."

Teen: "Well, it's just weird to think we could be brothers and we're both sitting here not knowing, and we'll leave and probably never find out."

Parent: "That's not only weird, I think it's sad."

Physical differences

Because adolescents' insecurity about their appearance is

heightened by any factor in which they perceive themselves to be different from others (breast size, penis size, height, weight, or complexion, for example), the physical ways in which they differ from their peers or from members of their adoptive family may concern them at this time in their lives.

In one family, the older child, a boy, was distressed that his younger sister was taller than he was. Not only did he believe boys should be taller than girls, but he felt that as the older sibling, he should be bigger.

Children with different biologic parents are likely to mature at different rates. That can be a source of jealousy and conflict in the family.

Telling teenagers that people develop differently, that they will catch up to their peers, or their peers will catch up to them is seldom reassuring to the teenager who is concerned with his appearance at that moment. Nevertheless, if you have information about his birthparents' growth and development, by all means share it with your adolescent.

When your teenager expresses unhappiness with his appearance, remember that this normal reaction may be exacerbated by his separation from the people he physically resembles. Don't deny his feelings, but encourage him to examine the evidence he is using to arrive at conclusions about his appearance.

Teen: "I'm so fat."

Parent: "You don't look fat to me, and I would tell you if I thought you were fat because it wouldn't be healthy and I'd want you to do something about it. But, that's just my opinion. What makes you think you're fat? Have you had to buy clothes lately that are a bigger size?"

You're not denying that he feels fat, but you are providing him with another viewpoint of the subject, and giving him some ways to test his perception against reality.

Finding physical role models

Adolescents' perceptions that they are physically different from their parents may leave them without the role models that teenagers generally look to in developing a sexual identity. This is particularly true for boys. They tend to see masculinity in terms of physical appearance more than girls, who traditionally associate femininity with nurturing.

One teenage boy, for example, wasn't athletic enough even for recreational sports, while his adoptive father's passion was watching boxing matches. As a result, the adoptee said he felt like a "sissy."

Teenagers' willingness to look to their adoptive parents as sexual role models may also be hampered if they believe sexuality is affected by infertility. It is difficult for children to think of their parents in sexual terms, and even more difficult if there are no biologic children to "prove" that their parents enjoy a sexual relationship.

Don't be concerned if your teenager develops a healthy relationship with a coach, teacher, Scout leader, church member, or other adult with whom he is more physically alike or who has a physical characteristic that seems to be important to your teenager, such as a muscular build.

Personality, abilities, and interests

"I don't know where she gets her interest in sports. Nobody in our family has ever played sports."

This comment could be made by either a biologic parent or by an adoptive parent. Scientists are still trying to discover how heredity and environment influence intelligence, personality, temperament, talents, and interests. But we do know that the combination of the two can result in children very different from their biologic parents or from the parents who raised them. Nevertheless, these differences and similarities are important to the adopted teenager who is trying

to discover how he is unique by comparing himself to his birthparents and adoptive parents.

A teenager may wonder (though not necessarily con-
sciously): "Why am I good at science? Did I inherit this ability
from someone? Did I become good at science to please my
parents who wanted a child who was good at science? Have I
ignored my abilities in other areas because I'm in a family of
scientists?"

He may have similar questions about his personality,
temperament, intelligence, abilities, talents, and interests.

For him to answer these questions, it is helpful to know
more about his birthparents and to imagine the kinds of expectations they might have held had they been able to raise
him. Even without this information, the teenager can use his
ability to think in scientific terms – formulating a hypothesis,
gathering evidence, and arriving at conclusions – to explore
this identity question.

A man adopted through donor insemination more than
forty years ago told me that he has always harbored a love for
music, but never learned to play an instrument. He is searching for his biologic father, and one of the questions he hopes
to answer is whether his biologic father is musically gifted. If
he is, that may be just the encouragement he has been looking
for all his life to pursue his own musical interests, he said.

Even though many biologic families have children whose
interests or abilities are different from those of the parents,
in an adoptive family, parents and teenagers may conclude
that the differences are due to adoption. Take care to let your
adolescent know you support his need to develop as a unique
individual. Don't assume, for example, that he knows he
doesn't have to be a minister just because you are. Let him
know that he is loved for his uniqueness, not in spite of it.

Teen: "I thought maybe I'd go out for cross-country this
    year."
Parent: "What makes you want to do that?"

Teen: "I just thought I'd try it."

Parent: "I hope you're not going to go out for cross-country because I like to run."

Teen: "No, but I knew you'd like it if I did."

Parent: "I'd enjoy running with you, and I'd enjoy watching you run. But I'll love you whether you go out for cross-country or not. I do what I enjoy, and I want you to do what you enjoy."

It may sound unnatural or even corny to tell a teenager you'll still love him if he makes a decision contrary to your preference, but it is important. It gives him freedom to make his own choices.

Teenagers may also find that people outside the family have expectations of them based on a family relationship that does not exist. For example, they may expect that if one person is a National Merit Scholar, the other children in the family will be, too, forgetting that heredity and environment influence intelligence.

An Asian–American child may encounter the expectation at school that he will be accomplished in math or science simply because he's Asian–American. But because he has not lived in an Asian family with its emphasis on education and respect for authority, he may not perform up to those expectations. And because identity is partially formed by perceiving how others see us, failing to live up to someone's expectations can result in a negative self-image.

Developing individual values and beliefs

Because adolescents can think in abstract terms, they can think about ideas, concepts, and values. And in their search for identity, they are likely to question whether their view of the world is their own or that of their parents. It isn't unusual

for the teenager to explore ideas and values different from the ones they've grown up with in an effort to answer this question.

This can be threatening to any parent, but may be even more so for an adoptive parent. For example, many teenagers question what gives their parents authority over them. When that question is asked in an adoptive family, it may rekindle earlier doubts that parents had about why they were entitled to be their child's parents.

Furthermore, parents who have played a nurturing role but not a biologic role in the growth and development of their children sometimes think "all" they have to offer their children are values. They may feel a sense of personal rejection if their teenager appears to reject their values. And when values are closely tied to membership in the family, as in religious beliefs, the feeling of rejection can be even greater.

New ways to think about things

When a teenager says, "I don't have to listen to you—you're not my real mother (or father)," he may be testing a concept that heretofore he's taken for granted—that the parent who has raised him, but isn't biologically related to him, is entitled to make rules for him.

Younger children obey rules because someone in authority told them they were rules and because they fear punishment for breaking them. Adolescents realize that rules don't just "exist" and authorities are not infallible. Consequently, they reason that they may not have to obey rules under some circumstances. They typically test what some of those circumstances might be, for example, whether parents have authority over their teenagers when they aren't at home.

The teenager may also be exploring another revelation of adolescence—that something has a particular name because we all agree on the meaning of that name. In this light, he may explore why he calls you "mother" or "father" when you are not biologically related. The answer may be that you are

his "parent" because you are committed to helping him grow and develop, and that commitment requires that you set limits for him.

It may be helpful to remember that a unique development in adolescence is the ability to argue from a position that the person doesn't necessarily agree with. So when the teenager says: "I don't have to listen to you — you're not my real mother (or father)," he is likely arguing it more from a hypothetical or philosophical standpoint than from a sense of conviction.

The appropriate response for the parent in this situation is to reinforce the idea that the parent is in charge:

Parent: "We're not talking about your adoption right now. We're talking about whether you can take the car without permission. You can't. And if you do, there will be consequences."

Later on, when the incident is over, it may be helpful for you to try to help the adolescent talk about rules, authority, and parents. Draw on the adolescent's new ability to see things from others' viewpoints in such discussions. Parents tell me they have more success when they communicate their interest in hearing their child's viewpoint rather than in driving home a point.

In starting such discussions, pick a time when you are both relaxed. It's often helpful to talk about the situation in terms of someone else other than your child. For example:

Parent: "Your Aunt Marilyn called me today. She just doesn't know what to do. She wants to marry Bill but she's afraid she's going to have hassles with his children."

Teen: "Why?"

Parent: "Well, the boys were visiting their dad this weekend and she asked one of them to clear the table after dinner and he just refused to do it. Bill told him

he had to do it, but it started a big fight and now
Marilyn is afraid that if they get married the boys
aren't going to accept her."

With a little forethought, you can lead your teenager to
express his views on the situation – why the boys might try to
challenge Aunt Marilyn's authority, what authority she has as
a stepmother, and how that authority might be perceived differently by children of different ages.

Don't feel you need to bridge that discussion to one about
your authority in your family or refer back to the earlier
discussion. You don't want your teenager to "learn a lesson";
you want him to practice discovering answers by seeing situations from different viewpoints. As his ability to do that im-
proves, he can arrive at the appropriate conclusions about
authority and rules in his own life.

Reconsidering religious values

Just as adolescents realize that rules don't just exist, they
come to look at religion differently than they did as a child.
Younger children believe they are Catholic because someone
told them they are or because they attend the Catholic
church. Adolescents realize that a person's religion is a reflection of his personal beliefs. Just as they re-evaluate other
aspects of their lives that they have accepted without questioning, teenagers are likely to test whether they really are a
Catholic or a Jew or a Lutheran or a Muslim. They may do
this through a healthy dialogue on religious issues, by refus-
ing to attend church or synagogue with their parents, or by
embracing other religions temporarily.

The question of religion can be even more confusing for
an adopted teenager if religion is considered part of being in
the family, as it would in families where religion and ethnic
origins are intertwined, such as in a Jewish, Muslim, or Irish–
Catholic family. In those cases, questioning religious beliefs
threatens their sense of membership in the family, which

adopted adolescents question anyway.

The adolescent may be thinking, for example:

"Am I really Jewish? I was converted to Judaism, attended the synagogue for 14 years, and was bar mitzvah, but I don't know if I believe all the things that Jews are supposed to believe. And how can I really be Jewish if my birthmother wasn't Jewish? If I hadn't been adopted by this family, I might have been adopted by a Christian or Moslem family. If my birthmother had kept me, I might have been a Catholic."

If we think about those questions as adults with presumably mature thought processes and are confused, think how troubling they can be for someone unused to thinking in those terms. No wonder the adolescent is in turmoil.

Try to think of this questioning of religious ideas as a time of growth for your adolescent. Take opportunities to talk about religious ideas, taking care not to argue for your own beliefs, but to explore philosophical ideas. One parent, for example, used news stories about religious–political events and medical ethics to stimulate such discussions and keep them from becoming too personal. It may be easier, for example, to talk about what "someone" should do if they are carrying a baby with a fatal inherited disease than to ask your teenager if she would ever have an abortion.

No matter how firmly you believe it, telling your teenager that he will suffer eternal consequences if he doesn't believe certain things will not convince him to believe what you believe. And it may cause a serious rift between you. Even though it seems at times that your adolescent wants nothing to do with his family, he desperately needs support and acceptance from his family during these difficult years. A parent could say, for example:

"You know how much I want you to believe in God. And

you know I think you'll find peace and guidance in religious study and participation. But this is something you're going to have to discover for yourself. I'll pray for you, but I know you'll have to make the decision to believe in God on your own."

Many parents take solace in knowing that after these turbulent adolescent years, most young adults return to organized religion, often to the religion in which they were raised.

Developing a family identity

Questions about family identity that arise as the adopted adolescent searches for his personal identity involve philosophical questions such as why his parents have authority over him (discussed earlier in this chapter), whether brothers and sisters can marry, whether he "owes" loyalty to his family or it must be earned, and more. Again, it isn't unusual for any adolescent to have these kinds of questions. Being adopted adds a dimension or a focus to them.

Some of these questions may be disturbing. You may not know the answers. Nevertheless, allow your teenager an opportunity to explore them. For example, lead the dinner table conversation to a discussion of a news event or local experience:

Parent: "I read today about a case in which a brother and sister who were adopted into the same family decided they wanted to get married. What do you think about that?"

Teen: "Gross."

Parent: "Why is it gross?"

Teen: "I can't wait till my brother leaves home."

Parent: "I'm not suggesting you and your brother get married, I just wondered whether you think a brother and sister should be allowed to get married."

Teen: "Isn't it against the law?"

Parent: "Yes. That's why these two people were in the news. They wanted to be an exception to the law. Why do you think the law exists?"

Teen: "Can't your children get a disease or something?"

Parent: "There's a slight increased risk of birth defects if the husband and wife are closely related genetically, as biologic brothers and sisters are. But if you're adopted, you aren't related genetically. So do you think it should be allowed?"

Teen: "Well, I guess, if they love each other."

Parent: "Why do you think people are shocked that this brother and sister, who say they love each other and aren't genetically related, want to get married?"

These kinds of questions are fascinating, and haven't been explored in much depth by our society. Furthermore, reproductive technology is advancing faster than the discussion of ethical and philosophical issues it raises. For example, a child conceived as a result of *in vitro* fertilization could have brothers or sisters who were conceived at the same time he was, but transplanted into other women, or frozen for later implantation. Listen to your teenager for clues about what he's thinking and help him examine those ideas by asking him provocative questions.

Dating fears

Many adults who have been adopted say that one of their biggest fears during adolescence was that they were unknowingly dating a birth relative. While this is unlikely to occur in traditional adoptions, particularly if care has been taken to place children outside their own communities, it has been known to happen. The important point is that teenagers believe it could happen.

However, dating a relative is a somewhat greater

possibility for those adopted through donor insemination, particularly if the doctor responsible for the inseminations used donors from the community. One biologic father told me he was shocked to see a television program in which a doctor said he had delivered two hundred children as a result of donor insemination – shocked because he believed he was this physician's only donor. This kind of situation emphasizes the need for greater openness in donor insemination – both in telling children they were adopted through donor insemination so they can be aware of the ramifications, and in providing adoptive families with access to identifying information about the birthfathers. (It also points to the need for some ethical determinations about how frequently a donor should be used.)

One adult told me that because she did not know she was adopted through donor insemination, she did not fear dating a relative during adolescence, but she and her teenage daughter have talked about her daughter's need to obtain a thorough social history of anyone she begins to date seriously to determine if the individual is possibly a first cousin.

As we saw earlier in this chapter, teenagers who worry about circumstances beyond their control can be helped to explore the actual difference those circumstances are making in their lives. Helping them do this is far more beneficial than minimizing their very real fears.

Generational continuity

One component of the adolescent quest for identity is the teen's desire to know who his "people" are – who he is connected to historically and genetically and what this means for him. Chapter 3 discusses how children who are adopted sometimes feel they have no extended family. They may not feel connected to anyone but their immediate adoptive family. This can be particularly troubling in adolescence when they begin to try to integrate their sense of being part of a "clan" into their personal identity. Are they "immigrant stock" because their adoptive family is? Are they "working class" because their birth family is? They will have to test these conditions against their own experience before they can consider them their own. This may involve rejecting values for a time, just as they might temporarily reject being Mormon to see if they are comfortable not being Mormon.

One adoptee, for example, found he was expected to attend the college his father, grandfather, and uncles had gone to. He chose a different school as a way of asserting his individuality.

Adolescents' entry into their reproductive years heightens interest in family identity as adolescents think about someday having children of their own. Their new understanding of genetics contributes to the awareness that they are connected genetically not only to their birthparents, but to a whole history of people.

Some of the academic subjects adolescents study in high school, such as biology and history, provide openings for talking about these issues. The death of a relative also can lead to discussions of inheritance, family heirlooms, and feelings about extended family.

Sometimes, simply allowing your teenager a chance to express his feelings, questions, or confusion about who his "people" are is enough to stimulate a discussion:

Parent: "Your grandfather gave me his gold watch when he died. His grandfather gave it to him on his wedding day. That was more than one hundred years ago. It will belong to you someday if you want it. I'd like you to have it, and I know grandpa would, too. How do you feel about owning it someday?"

Developing a racial or ethnic identity

One of the most urgent questions adoptees have when they search for their birthparents is: "What is my ethnic background?"

Our ethnic heritage is our connection to our historical and

genetic past. People who have been cut off from that past feel
as though they have sprung up from the earth, or arrived here
from an alien planet. They need a sense of connection.

In one family, the daughter felt uncomfortable with her
family's emphasis on its Italian roots until she learned her
birthmother was Italian.

In many families, the ethnic heritage of the family affects
the attitudes and values in that family. As with his religious
values, the adolescent adoptee may question to what extent
the view he has of the world is different because he was raised
by people of a particular ethnic heritage, and how it might
have been different if he had been raised by people who
shared his own ethnic heritage. He may wonder if certain personality characteristics and physical traits reflect his ethnic
background.

Try to elicit discussions of this issue by seizing appropriate opportunities to discuss it:

Parent: "Your birth family is Polish. How do you think
they might view the recent political events in Poland?"

Teen: "How would I know?"

Parent: "Well, let's say you have some distant relatives
still living in Poland. Would that make you more interested in the political events in Poland – perhaps increase your concern about how the government treats
workers?"

The adolescent who is transracially adopted

Adoptees who are racially different from their parents
experience questions of racial and ethnic identity to an even
greater degree. They know that if it had not been for their
adoption, they would have been raised in a culture, and
perhaps a country, far different from the culture in which
they were raised.

In Chapters 2, 3, and 5, we discuss how younger children
need to be proud of their cultural and historical roots and

need to feel comfortable as part of a minority group and a multi-racial family. Adolescents do not need more exposure to foods, customs, or travelogues of their birth culture. They need to understand how they fit into both the culture of their birth and the culture in which they were brought up. Do they "belong" with the Euro–American culture or the African–American culture? Should they only date other Hispanics? Are they accepted by their peers who share their racial background or by their peers who share their cultural background or neither one? One mother told me how her family had moved from a primarily Euro–American community to a large city so that their children could associate with other Asian–American teenagers. They found that because of the large number of Asian–Americans at the high school the children attended, the children were expected to associate only with other Asian–Americans. Having been raised in a Euro–American community by Euro–American parents, the children felt more comfortable with Euro–Americans and out-of-place at their new high school.

It is unrealistic to expect that an East Indian–American adolescent raised by Euro–American parents is going to think and feel the same way he would had he been raised by East Indian parents. Neither will he think and feel the same as he would if he were Euro–American. It may be that the obvious racial differences between him and his parents will enable the family to confront these identity issues more directly than in a family in which ethnic differences are not as obvious. For example, it could be more difficult for a teenager born to parents of Mediterranean extraction but brought up in a family descended from Eastern Europeans to confront his identity confusion than it is for an African–American teen raised by Euro–American parents. However, just because physical differences may make it easier to recognize ethnic issues, it doesn't mean it's easy being a transracially adopted teenager.

Cultural experimentation

During early adolescence, teenagers typically want to be as much like their peers as possible. So being racially different can be a problem. In fact, a certain amount of denial of racial differences is to be expected.

Some teenagers may want to "experiment" with different ethnic or racial cultures, "trying them on" as they do different religious beliefs or different styles of clothing. One Euro–American mother told me how her African–American son successfully bridges the cultural gap, adopting a manner of speaking, dressing, and carrying himself that is different depending on whether he is with his African–American or Euro–American friends. Your transracially adopted teenager may need a role model during these years who can help him understand what it means to be a member of a particular minority or who he perceives is better able to understand his feelings than you are.

As adolescents approach adulthood, they often want to explore their racial heritage more fully. Try to provide your older adolescent with opportunities to do so–a college that offers language, history, or literature courses pertaining to his birth culture, a trip to his country of birth after graduation from college, or a job in which he would have a chance to associate with people of his own race or birth culture.

One of my acquaintances told me that her son, who was raised in a Chinese family in the United States, refused to learn to speak Chinese or have anything to do with his family culture. After graduation from high school, he visited Taiwan. Once he had experienced being part of a majority culture instead of being in the minority, he became fascinated by his heritage and started to learn to speak Chinese.

Interracial relationships

Adoptees who have had friends of different racial or ethnic groups while growing up may find as they enter their dating years that cross-racial dating is unacceptable in their community, or that they are rejected by their friends. But transracially adopted teenagers may not feel comfortable with people of their own race because they have not been brought up in that culture.

And those teenagers who do date cross-racially may wonder whether the date represents a political statement or a sexual fantasy. I once heard an Asian–American woman recall how, as a teenager, she wondered whether boys asked her for dates because they truly liked her, or because they thought she was "exotic."

It may be difficult for your teenager to discuss this with you if you are not a member of a minority, because he may think, quite accurately, that you cannot empathize with his feelings of being rejected on the basis of race. It isn't necessary for you to tell your child you understand how he feels. Just let him tell you how he feels. As we discussed in Chapter 5, it is sometimes easier to help a child express his feelings by paraphrasing his own statements, rather than by questioning him. This is particularly true of adolescents, who may see questioning as "prying."

Parent: "Who are you taking to the dance?"

Teen: "I don't think I'm going to take anyone."

Parent: "You sound sad that you don't have a date for the dance."

Teen: "I asked Jaime, but she said she's going with her friends."

Parent: "So you're feeling that Jaime would rather go to the dance with her friends than with you."

Teen: "I think Jaime wants to go with me; it's her mother who doesn't want her to go out with me."

Parent: "You think her mother objects to you."

Teen: "She does."

Parent: "It sounds like you're angry that Jaime's mother objects to her going out with you."

Teen: "Well, she doesn't even know me. She just doesn't want her daughter to be seen with me because I'm Hispanic. She doesn't think I'm as good as they are or something."

Parent: "I can see why you'd be angry about that. It makes me angry, too. I think Jaime's going to miss out on a pretty good date, but I guess that's her problem."

Discussing racial issues

Television shows, movies, and news events often provide opportunities to talk about important issues in ways that allow teenagers to express their thoughts while still protecting their privacy because they can talk about situations other than their own.

For example, a television show featuring an Asian–American family can generate discussions of how Asian–American families are portrayed in the media and how realistic those portrayals are, giving your adolescent a chance to examine his perceptions of Asian–American families and compare them to the realities of his adoptive family and what he knows about his birth family.

A letter to the editor in the newspaper might prompt a discussion such as this one:

Parent: "There's a letter from the editor in tonight's paper saying the newspaper shouldn't have said the students who got into the fight at the pizza parlor were all from the African–American fraternity on campus. What do you think?"

Teen: "Everybody thinks if you're African–American you want to fight all the time."

Parent: "Is that true?"

Teen: "No, but people are always trying to pick a fight with me."

Parent: "Why do you think people want to fight you?"

Teen: "I don't know, but if I fight them, I know I'm going to get blamed for starting it, even if I didn't."

Parent: "What can you do about that?"

Teen: "Leave no witnesses . . . Just joking . . . I try to just walk away."

Assuming the birthparents' identity

Some teenagers, in their search for their identity, will adopt the identities of other people. In a small way, this is what teenagers are doing when they conform to each other in dress and personal appearance.

I am repeatedly asked whether teenage girls who are adopted will become pregnant to identify with their birth-mothers. Some apparently do. Some also seem to get preg-nant to live up to subtle messages from their adoptive parents that they expect their teenage daughter to repeat her birth-mother's experience.

The discomfort that many parents feel discussing sexual issues with their teenagers can be heightened in an adoptive family. Parents generally want to convey the importance of responsible sexual behavior to their teenagers. Yet doing so seems to be critical of the birthparents, or may imply that the teen's birth was undesirable. Parents can help their teenagers understand that they can learn from the experience of their birthparents, and that they have options the birthparents may not have been aware of.

Parent: "I heard that Cara is pregnant."

Teen: "Yeah. She's not due until August so she can prob-ably finish the school year."

Parent: "Surely Cara and Mike knew about birth control."

Teen: "Cara said it was the first time."

Parent: "Do you think it was?"

Teen: "Probably not."

Parent: "Some teenagers do get pregnant the first time they make love. But most of the time they don't. The fact is that if you're a teenager, there are probably going to be times when you want to make love, but a lot of teenagers aren't prepared for how strongly they are going to feel at those times. They think they will be able to control the situation, but they find out they're in over their heads. Then they think they can control it better the next time."

Teen: "They should have known that if Mike came over when Cara's parents were gone that they'd get into trouble."

Parent: "That's a good point. They let themselves get into situations where it would be difficult for them to stop. Once you make love with someone, it's hard to go back to having a relationship without that."

Teen: "They should have gotten some birth control."

Parent: "I think so, too."

Teens with little information about their birthparents, or with negative information about their birthparents, may worry that they will be like them in undesirable ways. I've heard of teenagers identifying with their birthparents by dressing in rags because they believe their birthparents are poor.

If your teenager seems to be identifying with his birthparents in undesirable ways, encourage him to look at contrary evidence about his birthparents and about himself. For example, if an adolescent boy is worried that he is going to be an inadequate father because his birthfather "abandoned" his birthmother during her pregnancy, a parent might discuss his concerns in this way:

Parent: "What do you mean, 'He abandoned her'?"

Teen: "When she got pregnant, he split. He didn't care

about her and he didn't care about me."

Parent: "Maybe there are other reasons he was not around when she was pregnant."

Teen: "If he really cared, he would have been there."

Parent: "What about your friend Rudy? When Stephanie found out she was pregnant, they broke up. Was that because he didn't care about her any more?"

Teen: "No, it was because Stephanie's parents wouldn't let him in the house any more."

Parent: "So, there might have been other reasons that your birthfather wasn't around."

Teen: "I guess."

Parent: "Let's imagine that he did care. What are some reasons that he might not have shown that?"

Teen: "Her parents could have been mad at him."

Parent: "Could he have run away from the problem because it seemed too big to face?"

Teen: "Yeah, but he should have stayed and helped my mother out."

Parent: "What would you do?"

Teen: "I'd stick by her. If her parents tried to keep me away from her, I'd find a way, if I really cared about her, even though I might be scared."

Parent: "So, you think you'd handle the situation differently from the way your birthfather did?"

Teen: "Yeah."

Parent: "I remember when dad cut himself with the chain saw. That must have been pretty scary for you, but you got him to the hospital and stayed with him until I got there. So, I think you would stick by your girlfriend or your wife when she was pregnant. Of course, if you don't feel ready to be a father, then you should be responsible about your sexual activity."

Sometimes adoptive parents expect teenagers to be like

their birthparents. One adoptive mother, who housed her daughter's birthmother during her pregnancy, reacted strongly whenever her daughter overate because the mother had not liked the eating habits she observed in the birthmother.

If you or your teenager truly expect him to behave a certain way because that is how his birthparent behaved, professional help may be necessary to resolve the issue.

Becoming independent

The self-evaluation of the teenager in his quest for identity leads him to greater independence as he develops his own values and gains experience making decisions by looking at situations from different viewpoints.

As he moves toward greater independence, the adolescent sometimes wants to be and will act like a dependent child. At other times, he wants to be treated as an independent adult. Similarly, the adolescent wants and needs to remain close to his family, but also wants to assert his independence. Unfortunately, parents don't always know when their adolescent wants to be a child and when he wants to be an adult. This unpredictability adds to the confusion and turmoil in the family with teenagers.

Imagine that you are a teenager. You want independence, but it scares you. You want the love and warmth that you've known growing up in your family, but you also want to move away from that family. What do you do?

Many teenagers look for warmth, love, security and independence in a romantic relationship – and quite appropriately. The intimacy that such a relationship brings, through the opportunity to share their most important thoughts and feelings, helps teenagers see themselves in realistic terms.

Imagine that you are a teenager who has the opportunity to have all the advantages of his family – warmth, security, love, acceptance – but without having to interact in a parent–child relationship. That may be how some teenagers view a relationship with their birthparents and may be one reason they want to have contact with their birthparents.

To an adolescent, a birth family who accepts him and loves him as he is may seem to be the emotionally safest place to turn as he moves away from the family he has known and from which he must assert his independence. He doesn't need to assert his independence from his birth family because he hasn't had dependent ties to them. In his birthparents he may hope to find exactly what he is looking for as an adolescent— parents who don't function as parents, who aren't setting down rules or telling him what to think or believe.

If you have had an open relationship with the birthparents throughout the adoption, it may be natural for the adolescent to turn to them at this time. This is like the adolescent who finds warmth and acceptance (but no hassles, curfews, or chores) in the family of a girlfriend or boyfriend.

When you feel jealous, which you probably will if you are normal, remember that your adolescent is not expressing a preference for his birth family, but a need to hang on to much of what he has found good about growing up in your family as he moves on to independence.

Chapter 7 discusses why it can be confusing for a teenager who doesn't already have a relationship with his birthparents to establish one during adolescence.

Emotional reactions to adoption in adolescence

Mourning something or someone that has been lost is done by people of all ages, from infancy to adulthood. The grief reaction that adopted children may have to the loss of their birthparents was initially discussed in Chapter 4 because it is during the middle childhood years that adopted children generally begin to realize they have lost significant people. They are likely to experience that sense of loss at other times of their lives, too, and continue to mourn.

We can hope that children who are encouraged throughout their development to ask questions and express their feelings about adoption and the loss of their birth-parents will not be overly disturbed during adolescence by the identity issues raised by adoption. But because individuals react in unique ways, no one can promise that. Some teen-agers will have strong emotional reactions to adoption, while others will not.

Just as the grief experienced during middle childhood is unlikely to be completely resolved at that time, but may sim-ply settle down a bit until it is triggered anew, grief is not necessarily resolved during adolescence, either.

Adoptees may go through periods in their adult lives in which they are confused, angry, depressed, ashamed, or otherwise burdened by unresolved emotional conflict con-nected to their adoptions.

Books such as *The Adoption Triangle: Sealed or Open Records: How They Affect Adoptees, Birth Parents, and Adop-tive Parents*, by Arthur D. Sorosky, Annette Baran, and Reuben Pannor (Garden City, N.Y.: Anchor Press/Doubleday, 1984), and *Lost and Found: The Adoption Experience*, by Betty Jean Lifton (New York: Harper & Row, 1988), describe the feelings of some adult adoptees, as do the autobiographi-cal accounts of adults who are adopted. (See the Activity at the end of Chapter 7.) They explain that feelings of loss con-nected to adoption are most likely to be triggered by other losses, such as divorce and death, by events closely associated with family, such as marriage and birth, or by concern over one's own health or the health of a child.

Conflict in adoptive families during adolescence

You may find that your teenager seems obsessed with be-ing adopted, or you may find him obsessed with a more "typical" adolescent issue, such as peer relationships. You may also find him equally concerned about a lot of different issues at once. Some adolescents will focus on one particular aspect of their lives, convinced that all their confusing feelings are due to this one issue. They may think that if they can only resolve that issue, the rest of their life will be smooth. Other teenagers see all aspects of their lives in confusion. One adopted adolescent may think all his problems are due to being adopted, while another might view all his problems as stemming from not having a car, and another might see adoption as one of many things causing him confusion.

The physical and mental changes that are disrupting your teenager's psychological equilibrium potentially affect all aspects of his life, even though he may only be focusing on one particular problem. Whatever you can do to help him use abstract thinking more comfortably will help his understanding of adoption as well as the other facets of his life.

Adoption is likely to be one of the topics you discuss with your teenager, but talking about drugs, school, friends, career choices, or anything else that seems to interest the adolescent will have a carry-over effect to understanding adoption because it helps the teenager make the transition from thinking about things like a child to thinking about them like an adult.

In families unrelated biologically, both adolescents and their parents may think they would agree more and understand one another better if they were biologically related. It's understandable that adolescents and their parents would like a simple explanation for the conflict they are having, so blame it all on adoption. Parents who have biologic children as well as adopted children may have an easier time understanding that conflict during adolescence is normal. Because individuals vary, not every adolescent will interact with his parents in the same way. It may be that in a family with both biologic and adopted children there is more conflict with the adopted teenager, but that's not necessarily because he's adopted.

One parent suggests dealing with normal adolescent-parent conflict by writing notes. For example:

"Dear Lisa,

I'm sorry I yelled at you in front of your friends. I know it embarrassed you, and you have a right to be angry about it. I was angry that you talked back to me in front of your friends, but my embarrassment and anger doesn't justify embarrassing you. I'll try to remember to speak to you privately when we have differences. I hope you will try to speak to me respectfully. I love you.

Mom."

Whether you write notes, have family meetings, or discuss issues privately, keep the lines of communication open during these adolescent years. Talk about whatever seems to interest your child. Be aware of events happening at your child's school and in your community so that you can use them to discuss meaningful issues. Try to determine what the best times are for discussions with your teenager – times when both of you will be relaxed and open to other viewpoints. Avoid trying to talk about important subjects immediately after your teenager has come home from school or when there's been conflict in the recent past. Even if the conflict has been between your teenager and someone else, and not between the two of you, he may be feeling angry and defensive, and not open to discussing important issues. Some parents find that mealtimes, bedtimes, and times spent traveling in the car are good times for discussions.

Activity: Joining an adoption group

Teenagers who have been adopted, and their parents, often benefit from sharing their thoughts and feelings with others like them. Even in families who communicate well, teenagers sometimes don't want to ask parents questions, share their feelings, or otherwise reveal their vulnerabilities. Parents often benefit from the experience of other parents.

Some adoption agencies and organizations have groups available for adoptive families with teenagers. Some are open groups in which new members can join as their need or interest arise. Others are closed groups which explore issues with the help of a facilitator for a defined period of time. Some groups are limited to families whose teenagers are having serious behavioral problems. Usually, teenagers meet separately from their parents, each group exploring its own issues.

Similar groups may be available for children adopted through donor insemination or surrogacy, for those adopted by single parents or stepparents, and others who share a unique way of joining a family.

If such a group is not available in your area, you may want to start one. It may be helpful to look at the way such groups have operated at Vista del Mar, a private adoption agency in Los Angeles with years of experience working with adopted teenagers and their parents.

Each group is limited to a small number of adoptive families. The adoptive parents meet separately from the teenagers. Two therapists meet with the parents weekly for the first four weeks with one therapist facilitating discussion and the other providing information. Then, one therapist meets with the parents while the other meets with the teenagers for the next four weeks.

Discussions in the parent group might focus on the concerns of a particular family, on specific adoption issues, or on general parenting issues such as discipline. All parents are encouraged to offer their opinions and insights.

In the teenagers' group, discussion topics include adoption issues and adolescent problems. The therapist tries to encourage the teenagers to express feelings they might not feel able to express with their parents or friends.

At the end, a joint session with parents and teenagers is held.

To start your own group:
- Find others with a similar interest. You may know people personally or find them through publicity efforts.

- Discuss the purpose for your group and how the group should be organized to achieve that purpose. For example, people may be more willing to share their feelings in a closed group because trust can be established in a way that is difficult if new people attend each meeting. You may want to have a closed group within an open group, for example, an organization for parents of adopted teenagers which periodically offers an intensive opportunity for families to explore issues in a limited, closed group. Or you may want to have a closed group for trans-racial adoptive families within a larger group.

- Discuss the rules for the group. Who can join? When can they join? What is the shared understanding of confidentiality? How often will you meet?

- Discuss the amount and kind of expertise or information you need to address the issues in your families. Are you looking for professional advice or group leadership, or are you interested in peer support? Will people be intimidated or more comfortable if a social worker or psychologist facilitates the group? Is the kind of expertise or information you need available? Perhaps you want to limit your group to parents, but you want to invite professionals to make presentations to you occasionally.

It would be ideal if such groups already exist in your community, led by professionals with years of experience with adoption issues. However, many people are well informed about issues, having gained expertise by reading and by attending some of the many conferences, workshops, and seminars offered.

It may be difficult to get your teenager to attend such a group with you, especially if the reason you want to attend the group is that you are experiencing a lot of conflict in your family. Approach your teenager by expressing *your* need for the group, not his:

> Parent: "There's a group of adoptive families meeting every Wednesday night for the next five weeks to talk about some of their feelings. The teenagers will meet in one room and the parents will meet in another room. I need to understand you better, and I think this will help me. Will you please come with me?"
>
> Teen: "I don't want to go to any adoption group."
>
> Parent: "I'm a little uncomfortable, too. But we don't have to say anything, and we don't even have to go back if we don't like the first session. But I want to understand you better, and I think if I listen to some other parents, we might not have as many arguments as we've had lately."

If your teenager is still resistant, suggest that he read the book *Who is David? The Story of an Adopted Adolescent and His Friends* by Evelyn Nerlove (New York: Child Welfare League of America, 1985). It describes the experiences of a teenage boy who participates in such a group, based on the author's experience leading such groups at Vista del Mar.

7. "I Want to Meet My Birthparents"

Adolescence

Don't be surprised if your adolescent wants to meet her birthparents. This desire has been described variously as normal curiosity and as a primal need to be reunited with the people to whom one is biologically related. Both descriptions are accurate, depending on the individuals and circumstances involved. One adoptee may at some time want to meet her birthparents out of curiosity and at another time to resolve a deep psychological need.

But the statement, "I want to meet my birthparents," doesn't always mean that's what the teenager wants. She may want to know what her birthmother looks like. She may be worried that she's dating a relative. She may have some medical concerns. She may be wondering what her birth was like. She may want to know what religion her birthparents' are.

Adolescents, who imagine that nearly everyone is as critical of them as they are of themselves, may also wonder whether their birthparents would approve of them or like them. Imagine how stressful it could be to wonder if you are acceptable to people you don't even know.

Your teenager may need your help identifying her real

need and the best way to meet that need. In some situations meeting her needs may involve immediate contact with birthparents. In other situations, it may involve postponing such a meeting but making contact by mail, telephone, or through an intermediary. Sometimes questions may be answered by a trip to the safe deposit box to read adoption documents or by talking about the teenager's concerns.

The desire to meet the birthparents

One way to help a teenager clarify the issue she's concerned about is to discuss a hypothetical meeting:

Parent: "If you did meet your birthmother, what do you think she would say to you after not seeing you for fifteen years?"

Teen: "My, how you've grown. That's what relatives always say."

Parent: "What would you say to her?"

Teen: "Why didn't you keep me?"

Parent: "You know, when I meet someone for the first time, I never know what to say to get a conversation going, but that question would sure do it."

Teen: "I wouldn't ask that first."

Parent: "Why not?"

Teen: "Well, we'd probably have to talk about what grade I'm in at school and whether I play any sports, and things like that first."

Parent: "You mean, kind of get to know each other before you get to the heavy stuff."

Teen: "Yeah."

Parent: "What kinds of things like that would you want to know about her?"

Teen: "Maybe whether she had any other kids; what her job is; whether she likes sports or my dad likes sports."

Parent: "How do you think your birthmother would be feeling while you talk about sports and school and things?"

Teen: "I think she'd be interested, but she might be feeling kind of nervous that I was going to hit her with a big question."

Parent: "You are. Do you think she knows what you're going to ask?"

Teen: "Probably. She's probably been thinking what she'd say if I ever showed up and asked her why she didn't keep me."

Parent: "Are there other questions you'd ask her? Other things you'd want to know?"

Teen: "Who's my birthfather?"

Parent: "Anything else?"

Teen: "No. That's what I want to know."

Parent: "Do you think if we went back to the agency and asked the social worker who placed you to explain why your birthmother didn't keep you and who your birthfather is that you'd be satisfied?"

Teen: "No, because my birthmother might have lied to her."

Parent: "So you think you'd have to get the answers from your birthmother to be able to believe them?"

Teen: "Yes."

Parent: "Would you like to write to your birthmother and ask her those questions?"

Teen: "How would we get a letter to her? And even if we did, she might not answer it."

Parent: "We could ask the adoption agency to send her the letter. And if we didn't hear from her, we'd have to decide what to do then. Why do you think she might not answer your letter?"

Teen: "Maybe she doesn't care about me. After all, she gave me away."

Parent: "I think your birthmother probably cares a lot about you, and thinks about you a lot, and would probably be delighted to hear from you. But if she weren't, would it be better to find that out by writing to her or by showing up on her doorstep one day?"

Teen: "If I showed up, she'd have to talk to me."

The teenager in this situation has some legitimate questions, and while she recognizes there are other ways to get those answers besides a meeting, she wants assurance that her questions will be answered – she wants control of the situation. She also appears to be dealing with some issues of rejection by her birthmother. She wants to know why she was placed for adoption, and she thinks the reason is that her birthmother didn't care about her. She's afraid her birthmother won't answer her letter because she still doesn't care about her. Knowing what her concerns are and why she wants a face-to-face meeting with her birthmother is helpful in deciding how her needs can best be met.

Natural curiosity

Teenagers need accurate information about their birth families to help them recognize the difference between reality and fantasy, to reassure them, and for positive identity formation (identity formation is discussed in Chapter 6). The information teenagers need includes:

- the physical aspects of their birthparents, including inheritable conditions;

- the birthparents' personalities, interests, talents, and abilities;

- the circumstances of their birth and the reason their birthparents terminated their parental rights;

• their birthparents' race or ethnic background and facts about their extended family.

Many parents do not have all this information to provide their teenagers when they have questions about their birthparents. But even if they do – even if they have a full medical, psychological, social, and family history of both birthparents, the adoptee might still say: "But I want to meet them."

To understand this, think back to the days when you were deciding whether to add to your family a child who was unrelated to you. You might have been given a fact sheet about the child and her birthparents. You might have had a fact sheet to which personal comments were added, such as, "likes to play with a yellow daisy rattle." Maybe you had a photograph. You might have had a letter from the birthparents or been able to talk to someone who knew the birthparents. Perhaps you had the opportunity to meet the birthparents and develop a relationship.

The more personal the information, the more meaningful it probably seemed. And information we gather ourselves often seems more reliable to us. If we asked the birthmother, "Why aren't you going to keep this baby?" her reply is more meaningful because we could hear her voice, see her facial expression, and feel her emotional response. Hearing someone describe our baby is more meaningful than seeing a picture, but seeing her ourselves is more meaningful yet.

So an adoptee's desire to meet her birthparents may be an attempt to personally gather information, even though she may already have detailed information on paper. Many teenagers say that what they would really like is to be a "fly on the wall" in their birthparents' homes. They'd like to be able to observe their birthparents without being detected so they could obtain the information they want without having to be involved in a relationship.

Other reasons for wanting a meeting

Some teenagers do want to get to know their birth-parents and to have the birthparents get to know them. For some, this could be an extension of the information-gathering process – an awareness that their understanding of their birthparents (and therefore themselves) will be deeper and more reliable if they get to know each other in an emotionally intimate way.

Adolescents may also want a relationship with their birth-parents and other members of their birth family to develop a connection with their past and with their historical and racial "people."

Other teenagers may want to develop a relationship with their birthparents because they have idealized them and think they would be better parents than the parents they have. For example, one teen wanted a mother who was more physically demonstrative in expressing affection. She imagined her birthmother would be this way.

A teenager adopted through donor insemination wanted to find her birthfather because she and her adoptive father were having a lot of conflict and she wanted to believe she was not to blame for it – that it was simply the result of a biologic "mismatch."

Of course, because teenagers often rebel against a decision of their parents, some express a strong desire to meet their birthparents because their adoptive parents have made it clear they won't be allowed to.

Some adoptees describe a deep longing to be reunited with their birthparents. One adoptee described the longing as a desire to find the piece of her that was missing so that she could feel whole. Sometimes this longing is explained as a need arising out of the "bonding" that took place between the adoptee and the birthmother prenatally and during childbirth. While bonding doesn't work quite that way, some adoptees do have a stronger desire for contact with their birthparents than others. This need is so profound that they may not be able to find psychological peace until they have satisfied the need.

Open adoptions

In many open adoptions, the adoptive family develops a relationship with the birthparents at the time of placement, and the two families "grow" together. Open adoptions are so new that we don't have much experience with adolescents who have had ongoing relationships with their birthparents. Theoretically, open adoptions eliminate the awkwardness of having to define roles and establish new relationships before an adolescent can obtain information from her birthparents. Those roles will have evolved over time, and everyone involved will know what those roles are. Usually, adoptive parents have a relationship with their child's birthparents similar to those they have with close adult friends with whom they share a common interest. Seldom do the adoptive parents and birthparents "co-parent" the child as she grows up.

In such a situation, in which the relationship between the adoptee and the birthparents has been established for a long time, the birthparents can be very helpful to the adoptee as she strives for her own identity and independence. Not only can they provide her with information, but they can be people who love her and whom she can trust. The birthparents come without the "baggage" that she has with her adoptive parents – that is, the conflict that is normal for parents and teenagers to have.

In an adoption in which the adoptive parents and birthparents have not maintained a relationship, but in which the identity of the birthparents can be easily determined, setting up a reunion may not be difficult, but it may be undesirable during adolescence.

Disadvantages of reunions in adolescence

Even experts who are strongly in favor of adoptees and birthparents having access to their birth records and advocate making all adoptions "open" caution against adolescents searching for birthparents they haven't seen since their placement. They recommend that the adoptee wait until adulthood for this reunion.

Unless an adoptee knows who her birthparents are and how to contact them, searching for them is time-consuming, expensive, and energy-draining.

But even when it's as easy as picking up the phone to make contact, establishing a relationship with a birthparent during adolescence can raise more issues than it resolves. It will be confusing for a teenager to begin a relationship with "parents" at the very same time she is desperately trying to become independent from her parents.

To their credit, most birthparents who meet their adolescent child will say, "I don't want to be your father (or mother). You already have parents who have done an excellent job raising you. I want to be your friend." But the teenager may not have any models for friendship with an adult, particularly an adult to whom she is related. Most adults in her life have been authority figures.

While adolescents can understand that two sets of people can both be called "parents," but have different roles, living with this can be confusing. If the adolescent and the birthparent are not going to relate to each other as the teenager has learned parents and children relate to each other, then how are they going to relate? It's going to involve some trial and error before they can establish a smooth and meaningful relationship.

From the birthparents' standpoint, however determined they may be to play a responsible role with their teenage child, it may be very difficult not to function in parental roles when dealing with a teenager who is at a stage of development when she is seeking answers to questions and direction to her life.

One birthfather described to me how he offered his daughter advice on which college to attend, even requesting that information on programs be sent to her. He meant his help to be that of a friend, but it could easily have been interpreted as parental interference.

It is far easier to establish a meaningful relationship with birthparents when the adoptee has completed the tasks of adolescence and is ready to form adult relationships. Some older teenagers may be ready to form such relationships. Others may not be ready to do so until much later.

Discouraging reunions

While parents may be able to see that a meeting between the teenager and her birthparents might cause more confusion for the adolescent than it resolves, the teen may not. In this situation, if parents refuse to allow a meeting, the teenager, who wants to be treated like an adult who can make her own decisions, may rebel.

The best resolution of this situation is for the adolescent herself to decide to postpone such a meeting. Encourage your teenager to look at the situation from different perspectives and evaluate what might be gained or lost by such a meeting. Help her focus on what her reasons are for wanting such a meeting and encourage her to explore other ways of meeting those needs.

Parent: "Why do you want to meet your birthmother?"

Teen: "I want to know what she looks like. I want to ask her some questions. I want to see if I have any brothers or sisters—lots of reasons."

Parent: "I know those are important questions and I can see why you would want to have them answered. Do you suppose your birthmother has some questions, too, that she'd like answered?"

Teen: "Like what?"

Parent: "What do you think they might be?"

Teen: "Do I hate her for giving me away?"

Parent: "If you think someone might hate you for something you did, how do you find out whether they do or not?"

Teen: "You can ask them."

Parent: "And if you think someone hates you, but they say, no, they don't, do you usually feel better right away?"

Teen: "What they say isn't as important as how they act toward you. You'd have to wait and see if they acted like they liked you."

Parent: "How do you think you'd have to act to convince your birthmother that you don't hate her?"

Teen: "She might want me to call her on the phone every week or every night, come visit her on the weekend, send her a birthday card—stuff like that."

Parent: "Is that what you want to do? Are you ready for that?"

You should also discuss the possibility of rejection and disappointment if the still hypothetical meeting didn't turn out the way the teenager hoped it would, for example:

Parent: "I think your birthmother has probably wondered about you all these years and would want to see you, but how would you feel if you called your birthmother and she said she didn't want to talk to you or see you?"

In discussing whether she should have a meeting with her birthparents, try to convey that it is a complicated issue that must be thoroughly examined before a decision is made. It isn't something that can be worked through overnight. Let her know you are open to the idea of a meeting, but explain that you expect her to be open to the idea that maybe this isn't the best time for a meeting.

Through your discussions, get a feel for what your teenager's needs are and whether they can be satisfied by anything other than an actual meeting. Try to determine how intensely she feels she needs a meeting at this time. And assess whether your teenager is mature enough to handle such a meeting.

Remember that when a teenager says, "I want to meet my birthmother," she may not know how to say what she really needs. Maybe all she needs is some information. Maybe she needs a letter or phone call from her. Maybe she really does need a meeting. The important thing is to decide together what her real needs are and how they can be met in a way that is in her best interests.

Resolving an impasse

If after thorough discussion your teenager still wants a meeting, but you have determined that it is not a good idea at this time—what can you do? After all, forbidding such a meeting will likely result in rebellion, but you don't want to agree to something that you really believe is not in your teenager's best interests.

Clearly, you have a situation in which neither option is acceptable. As a last resort, you might want to get the birthparent involved in the decision-making. You could try contacting the birthparent, discussing with her the reasons your teenager wants to meet with her and the reasons you think such a meeting should be postponed. Ask for her cooperation in trying to resolve the dilemma. If you haven't had contact with the birthparent before or in a while, you will probably need the assistance of a third party to negotiate a solution. When you've reached agreement, you can tell your child that you and her birthparents have discussed it and agree that it would not be a good time for them to have a meeting, but that they are willing to meet with her at a later date, and in the meanwhile, she will be provided with the answers to whatever questions she has, through an intermediary. It may be advisable not only for you to say this, but for the birthparent to reinforce it independently, perhaps through a letter. A teenager may be less likely to conclude that her adoptive parents are obstructing a meeting if she receives a letter from her birthparents saying, "I want to meet you, too, and it is really hard for me to wait, but I made a hard decision once before to be separated from you because I thought it was best for you. And I think it's best for you if we delay our meeting for a little while longer."

How successful you are in engaging the cooperation of the birthparents depends on how you approach them as well as unpredictable factors such as the kinds of life decisions they are facing at the time.

Feelings of adoptive parents

Some adoptive parents resist a meeting between their teenager and her birthparents under any circumstances. If your teenager has been idealizing her birthparents and finding fault with you, you may be feeling jealous. Or a parent may fear that if the teenager has contact with her birthparents she will stop loving her adoptive parents. In other words, they may mistakenly view her interest in her birthparents as a rejection of them.

Furthermore, while parents want their children to grow up and become self-sufficient, it is tough for all parents to see their children becoming independent because it means they will need their parents less, and everyone likes to feel needed. Parents who have no biologic ties to their children may wonder what kind of relationship they will have with their child when their nurturing role is over. This insecurity may be heightened by the desire of the teenager to be reunited with her birthparents. It may seem to confirm the adoptive parents' fear that once their nurturing role is over, the child will return to her biologic family.

One researcher told me that he's observed that adoptive parents whose sons and daughters are in their thirties are more sincerely supportive of the adoptees' desire to search for their birthparents than those whose children are still adolescents or young adults. It may be that parents whose sons and daughters are grown feel more secure in their relationship than those whose children are on the verge of adulthood.

Adoptive parents who are concerned about their teenagers having contact with their birthparents may find it helpful to recognize the reasons teenagers may want contact, as well as the reasons they may be idealizing their birthparents and criticizing their adoptive parents (see "Idealizing the birthparents" in Chapter 6). Parents may want to read some of the accounts of reunions written by adoptees (see the Activity section at the end of this chapter) to see that the desire for reunions do not arise out of rejection of the adoptive parents. In most cases, the adoptee's relationship with her adoptive parents is enhanced rather than diminished by contact with her birthparents. Adoptive parents may want to seek support from other parents whose teenagers have wanted to have contact with their birthparents through an adoption or stepparent support group.

Decisions made out of fear or a sense of impotence are generally not well considered. Adoptive parents shouldn't agree to let their teenager meet her birthparents because they think they don't have the right to keep them apart. Nor should they prohibit a meeting because they fear the loss of their adolescent's love if she is reunited with her birthparents. If you feel you are making a decision about your teenager's contact with her birthparents based more on your needs than on your teenager's, get counseling from someone knowledgeable about adoption issues.

Planning a reunion

If everyone agrees that face-to-face contact is desirable at this time, take the time necessary for everyone to be prepared for the meeting. This often requires the assistance of a negotiator. All participants should understand:

- What their roles will be with the people they are about to meet and what kinds of responsibilities, privileges, and limitations there are to those roles. For example, does the birthmother now expect to be invited to the adoptee's birthday celebration?

- How communication is to be handled. Will it be handled directly or through an intermediary? Must the adoptive parents be consulted before the adoptee contacts her birthparents or the birthparents contact the adoptee?

- How conflict will be resolved. What if the adoptive parents and the birthparents disagree about the amount of contact? About values? About decisions the adoptee is making?

Everyone involved should identify the fears and hopes each has about the teenager's contact with her birthparents so expectations can be realistic. The adoptee needs to be prepared for disappointment and rejection if her fantasies about contact with her birthparents are not realized, as do the birthparents. The adoptee and her adoptive parents need to be prepared for the effects this new relationship may have on their established relationship – the adoptive parents may feel jealous, or the adoptee may develop a new appreciation for her parents. The more prepared everyone is for this new relationship, the more smoothly its establishment is likely to go.

Parent: "I know you've thought a lot about what your

birthmother will be like. Have you considered that she might not be what you expect?"

Teen: "What do you mean?"

Parent: "For example, you want to know whether you have any brothers or sisters and who your birthfather is. How will you feel if she won't tell you?"

Teen: "Why wouldn't she tell me?"

Parent: "Maybe she never told your birthfather she was pregnant."

Teen: "I still have a right to know who he is."

Parent: "I agree. But what will you do if she doesn't?"

Moving in with the birthparent

"What if I want to live with my birthmother?"

Teenagers do not really want another set of parents. But because they compare their parents to other adults and generally conclude that any other adult would be better than the parents they're living with, they may think that life would be easier if they lived with a different parent. When that is a real possibility because there is another parent with whom the teenager doesn't currently live, she may demand to live with that parent.

Parents can use the same techniques they've used before to resolve conflict in this situation. Through discussion, try to get your adolescent to see realistically what the situation might be like and conclude on her own that she doesn't really want to move. You can also involve the birthparent in the process, who might say to the teenager, "We both agree that it's best for you to live with your adoptive parents."

Outright refusal is likely to provoke rebellion and conflict, but if you really don't think living with her birthparents is in her best interests, it may be your only alternative.

Some adoptive parents have allowed their teenager to

move in with her birthparents to let her find out first-hand that it isn't a decision she'll like. There may be extreme situations in which this is the only solution. But parents should only allow their teenager to live with another parent if they are convinced that such a move is in the teenager's long-range interests – not just a way to avoid conflict or "learn a lesson."

If you are not going to allow your adolescent to live with her birthparents, try to set up some alternatives that would allow your teenager a lot of freedom in her relationship with her birthparents and a lot of contact with them, assuming that the birthparents are people with whom you feel comfortable allowing your teenager to be. For example, you might allow her to stay overnight on occasion, or to go on a short trip with the birthparents.

When birthparents initiate a meeting

On occasion, birthparents may contact the adoptive family when the adoptee is an adolescent and request a face-to-face meeting. Most birthparents, out of respect for the adoptive parents, will contact the parents before contacting the adoptee to ask for permission.

If you are contacted by a birthparent, request some time to sort through your own reactions and plan how to deal with the request. During this time you might talk with your teenager about how she would feel if her birthparent suddenly wanted to meet her. (Of course, if you haven't been having discussions like this all along, your teenager is going to suspect the real reason for your inquiry.)

Also, discuss with the birthparent the possibility that adolescence may not be a good time *for the adoptee* to have a face-to-face meeting. Try to agree on the process that will be used to reach a decision on whether to have a meeting.

Even if you and the birthparent agree that a meeting now would not be advisable, I think the adoptee has a right to know that contact with her birthparents, which she may have thought impossible, is now possible. Involve her in the decision-making process as you would if the request for contact came from her.

This is going to make your situation more complicated than if you just allowed the birthparent to quietly disappear again. But the birthparent is not going to disappear. The birthparent will probably contact the adoptee when she is older. If he says, "I contacted your parents when you were fifteen, but we agreed that wouldn't be a good time for us to meet," the adoptee may be very angry that she was deceived into thinking it was impossible for her to have contact with her birthparents.

While a face-to-face meeting may not be desirable, having some kind of contact with birthparents may be very advantageous for the adolescent who is struggling with identity issues.

If you have an eager or impatient birthparent who is reluctant to give you the time you need to work through your thoughts, help your teenager make a decision, and prepare for the possibility of a meeting, remember that the birthparent may have invested a lot of time, money, and emotional energy to find the adoptee. It may seem impossible for the birthparent to wait any longer to see the adoptee. You can hope that the birthparent would respect your need for time, but he may not. He is more likely to respect a request from the adoptee to have a little time to sort through her thoughts and feelings before having a meeting.

If your adolescent decides against a meeting, make sure she finds a good way to tell the birthparent so that the birthparent isn't left thinking you obstructed a meeting. Try to negotiate an alternative that will allow the birthparent and the teenager to have some contact, perhaps by letter, that both can feel comfortable with.

A final note

Don't get involved in deceptions like secretly inviting your adolescent's birthparents to her high school graduation, or arranging for your teenager to take a job where her birthparent works.

While these might seem like ideal ways for the birthparent to get the reassurance he needs, or the adoptee to get the information she needs without the confusion of entering into a new relationship during adolescence, deception is never good for relationships. Deal with the situation openly.

Parents who treat their adolescents with respect—discussing issues rather than dictating, actively listening to their opinions, allowing them to express their feelings and preferences, and respecting their need for privacy and independence—are often surprised with the maturity with which they make decisions.

Activity: Reading about search and reunion

The following books are helpful in understanding the need adoptees have for contact with their birthparents:

Lost & Found: The Adoption Experience, rev. ed. by Betty Jean Lifton (New York: Harper & Row, 1988).

Based on the author's own experience and her contact with other adoptees, this book provides insight into what it is like to be adopted and the motivations of those who search. The 1988 edition includes an extensive resource section, which includes state-by-state lists of support groups, agencies favoring open adoption practices, and therapists knowledgeable about adoption issues, as well as national registries and organizations.

The Adoption Triangle: Sealed or Open Records: How They Affect Adoptees, Birth Parents, and Adoptive Parents, rev. ed. by Arthur D. Sorosky, Annette Baran, and Reuben Pannor (Garden City, N.Y.: Anchor Press/Doubleday, 1984).

One of the most comprehensive books on the effects of search and reunion on adoptees, adoptive parents, and birth-parents, it includes a resource list of organizations involved in adoption and in search and reunion.

In Search of Origins: The Experience of Adopted People, by John Triseliotis (Boston: Routledge & Kegan Paul, 1973).

An insightful report of seventy adoptees who requested information about their birth relatives in Edinburgh, Scotland.

There are many first-person accounts of searching by adoptees. The following are particularly helpful:

Twice Born: Memoirs of an Adopted Daughter, by Betty Jean Lifton (New York: McGraw-Hill, 1975; New York: Penguin Books, 1977).

Betty Jean Lifton, who is an outspoken advocate for open records, tells her own story of searching for her birthmother before it was a common practice. It is a balanced account, and one of the best.

The Search for Anna Fisher, by Florence Fisher (New York: Arthur Fields Books, Inc., 1973).

In one of the first autobiographical accounts of an adoptee who searches for and finds her biologic parents, Florence Fisher recounts her twenty-year effort to find her biologic parents and the founding of ALMA (Adoptees' Liberty Movement Association), which provides information and support to those who search.

Searching for Minors, comp. by Mary Jo Rillera (Np., 1982). (Available from Triadoption Publications, P.O. Box 638, Westminster, Calif. 92684.)

Contains accounts by birthparents and adoptive parents, and a few adoptees, of contact between birthparents and adoptees when the adoptees were still minors.

Faces of Adoption, rev. ed. by E. Lynn Giddens (Chapel Hill, N.C.: Amberly Publications, 1984). (Available from Amberly Publications, P.O. Box 4153, Chapel Hill, N.C. 27515-4153.)

Through personal stories, relates the need adoptees have for information about their biologic relatives.

A Time to Search, ed. by Henry Ehrlich (New York: Paddington Press, 1977).

Adoptees tell their own stories of searching for their birthparents, including why they were motivated to search.

Dialogue for Understanding I (Palo Alto, Calif.: Post Adoption Center for Education and Research, 1981) and *Dialogue for Understanding II: Women's Voices* (Oakland, Calif.: Post Adoption Center for Education and Research, 1984).

Provides personal accounts by adoptive parents, adoptees, and birthparents about their experiences with adoption, including the need for information about biologic relatives. (Available from Post Adoption Center for Education and Research, 2255 Ygnacio Valley Road, Suite L, Walnut Creek, Calif. 94598.)

How It Feels To Be Adopted, by Jill Krementz (New York: Alfred A. Knopf, 1982).

Nineteen children ages eight to sixteen describe their feelings about adoption, including their thoughts about their birthparents. Some of the children have been contacted by their birthparents.

See also the list of fiction books for adolescents in Appendix B: Bibliography of Children's Books.

8. "Why Didn't You Tell Me?"

Children have a right to know how they joined their families and should learn this early. Parents today who go to court to adopt their children generally tell the children at an early age that they are adopted. But I still hear about families who have not told their children that they are adopted – in one case, not sharing that important information despite the probability that the birthparent would soon contact the child directly.

Adoption is more likely to be kept a secret when children are born into their families and adopted by a stepfather, or are adopted through donor insemination or *in vitro* fertilization. Indeed, the advice to families who have adopted through donor insemination has been to keep the child's true paternity a secret. Only recently, through books such as *Having Your Baby By Donor Insemination*, by Elizabeth Noble (Boston: Houghton Mifflin Co., 1987), and *Lethal Secrets: The Shocking Consequences and Unsolved Problems of Artificial Insemination*, by Annette Baran and Reuben Pannor (New York: Warner Books, 1989), and organizations such as Donors' Offspring (P.O. Box 33, Sarcoxie, Mo. 64862), has there been a change in attitude toward more openness in families formed through donor insemination.

The harm of secrecy

Chapter 1 explains that it is important to tell children they are adopted because children have a right to the truth about themselves. Enduring relationships are built on honesty, not deception. When there has been secrecy in a family about adoption, everyone suffers.

One man adopted through donor insemination said secrecy "poisoned" the relationships in his family, particularly between his mother and adoptive father. They were afraid to go out together, he said, because they might encounter comments about how different their sons were from them. This man was very close to his younger brother until he was twenty-one, when they began to drift apart. Years later he learned their relationship changed when his brother discovered they were both adopted through donor insemination and was persuaded to keep that information from his older brother.

Adoptees I have talked to seldom say the revelation that they were adopted was a surprise. They generally had a sense of being different from others in the family, or an awareness of a secret in the family about them. Once they learned they were adopted, a lot of confusion in their lives was resolved. One man, whose parents were not well-educated, was surprised to find himself in advanced placement classes in high school. He couldn't understand how he could be so intelligent when his parents were not, and worried about the time when he would be revealed as a fake.

For some, the effects of having their suspicions of adoption denied are long-term. When children are consistently told that a situation is different from the way they perceive it, they often learn not to trust themselves or others. Because she was told growing up that she was imagining differences that were real, one adoptee said she now never trusts what people tell her.

Revealing the adoption

Parents who conceal a child's adoption from him do not intend to be malicious or insensitive. Perhaps they intended to tell the child when he was seven or eight, but weren't quite sure how, and consequently, never did. Sometimes they conceal the facts because they mistakenly believe the child is "better off" not knowing.

Later on, the child may ask a question so pointed that the parents cannot bring themselves to conceal his history, or the parents become informed about the need of a child to know his origins. Perhaps fear that someone outside the family will reveal the secret convinces the parents to tell the child how he joined the family.

It isn't easy. Besides having to suddenly deal with all the issues surrounding being adopted, children whose adoption is revealed to them at an older age must also deal with their feelings about having been led to believe something about themselves that was false.

Whatever the reasons were for not telling the truth about how a child joined the family, they probably are all some form of protecting the child—for example, protecting him from feelings of rejection by his birthparents or by members of his extended adoptive family, protecting him from some negative information about his birth family or his origins, or protecting him from feeling "different."

We do need to protect our children at times, for example, by fencing in a yard because we can't trust a toddler to keep out of the street. But when we try to protect people's feelings, we're saying we think they are incapable of dealing with their feelings themselves.

There's a difference between not wanting our children to feel any sadness or hurt and keeping them from feeling sad or hurt because we don't think they can deal with those feelings. Adoption, like many other situations in life, involves sadness and pain. But most children who are brought up in emotionally healthy families learn how to deal with these kinds of feelings.

Telling a child the truth about his origins needn't mean confusing him or damaging his self-esteem. It means providing age-appropriate information in an emotionally supportive environment.

Although parents probably sincerely thought it would be best for the child to think of them as his biologic parents, it probably served the parents' interests as well to keep the truth a secret. It's important to recognize this because when parents tell the child of his adoption, he may have difficulty seeing how his parents could have thought it was in his best interests not to know the truth about his origins and may focus on how the secret benefited them.

It isn't unusual for parents to wish they shared a genetic and family history with a child whom they deeply love. This wish can lead to pretending the child is their biologic child. Particularly when a child was conceived by donor insemination or *in vitro* fertilization with a donor egg or embryo, it is easy for parents to pretend the child is their biologic child, especially if either parent feels infertility takes away from their masculinity or femininity. Some adoptive parents have felt they were "letting down" their family by not producing a one hundred percent genetic heir, or felt family members would have been critical of the way they formed their family.

It's possible that what parents "gained" by not being honest about a child's adoption was a reprieve from dealing with some infertility issues. If that is your situation, you may want to address those issues now. Resolve, Inc. (see Appendix A: "Do We Need More Help?"), is available to provide ongoing support and information to infertile couples. Their help is not limited to people in the early stages of infertility.

Sometimes protecting our children from sadness or pain

is a way of protecting ourselves. We don't want our child to feel bad because we don't know what to do with a child who is in pain. It hurts us to see our child suffer. All parents feel this way to some degree, but some people feel *responsible* for other people's feelings. They believe they are responsible for the people around them being happy. Their own feelings seem to be controlled by the feelings of those around them – they can't be happy unless those around them are happy, so they try to insure that those around them will be happy. If this seems to be at the core of your wanting to protect your child from the sadness and pain of adoption, you might want to read books about this condition, called "codependency." One excellent book is *Codependent No More*, by Melody Beattie (New York: Harper & Row, 1987). Your community may have a support group for codependents, including Al-Anon. (Codependency was first recognized in those living with alcoholics, but Al-Anon is open to other codependents as well.) You might also want to consider individual counseling.

Understanding the importance of honesty

If you have not yet told your child the truth about his adoption, it is important to understand why you think it would be best for your child to know the truth now. This under-standing addresses the issue of whether you are telling your child the truth because you have to or because you want to. If you don't want to tell him the truth, it may be difficult for you to confront your own feelings about his adoption, to work through the issues necessary to developing open communica-tion on the topic, and to be supportive as he works through the issues.

Whatever the initial motivation, you must come to the conclusion that it is best for your child to know the truth if you are going to be able to help him work through the issues, and if the secret, once revealed, is not going to harm your relationship.

Find out as much as you can about the feelings and questions of adoptees so that you can better understand their need to know the truth about their origins. James Stingley's book *Mother, Mother* (New York: Congdon & Lattés, 1981), discusses the intense emotional reactions the author had to learning as an adult that his father deliberately arranged to impregnate a woman he and his infertile wife had befriended with the intention of then coming to her aid by adopting the child.

Emotional reactions to revealing the secret

Adoptees often have strong reactions to learning that while they were kept in the dark about their origins, others knew the truth. Imagine how you would feel if someone had been keeping vital information from you. Imagine how you would feel if this secret was kept not just by your parents, but by people outside the family. You might rightly feel you were the victim of a conspiracy. Your child may be angry at you not only for keeping him in the dark about his origins, but for sharing information that rightly belongs to him with other people. And he may also be angry with them for cooperating in the deception.

Furthermore, the more people who know the secret of the child's origins, the more likely it is that it is not really a secret – that the child actually knows or is highly suspicious.

Though you may feel threatened at the thought of revealing the truth – and, in fact, your relationship with your child may be threatened by that deception – there is still potential for a much deeper relationship founded on truth.

If you are going to reveal a child's adoption to him after years of telling him another story, get a third party involved – a therapist, social worker, or other qualified counselor on adoption and family issues. You will have issues to work through, and your child will face adoption issues that he never considered before.

The information in this book can help you understand what your child is likely to understand about adoption at a given age. But remember, if your child is twelve, he will have to work through not only the adoption issues that twelve-year-olds face, but all the issues that he should have dealt with before that time.

You also may have to rebuild a damaged relationship with your child. And you and your child are probably going to feel grief at the loss of the fantasy you have both had that he is your biologic child.

Because the issues your family are dealing with are new and complex, you may need help sorting them out. Don't feel you have to do this alone. Get help, and get help from someone familiar with infertility and adoption issues. (See Appendix A: "Do We Need More Help?" for suggestions of how to find counselors knowledgeable about adoption issues.)

Telling the story

If you have fabricated a story about how your child joined your family, telling the real story will be, at best, awkward. If you wait for a time or a situation that seems ideal, you may continue to put off telling the truth. In fact, one reason you may not have told the truth already is because you were waiting for a time or situation in which you could tell the truth without your child feeling sad or hurt or rejected, or without you feeling embarrassed, sad or anxious. Remember, even if you had been telling your child the truth all along, there would have been times when talking about how your child joined your family was awkward, sad, embarrassing, or painful.

Try to understand the issues your child will be facing and the issues you will be facing once the truth is revealed. And consider how you will present the child's adoption in a positive way. This is especially important if you are revealing the story involuntarily, for example, because a birthparent is about to make contact with the child. If you have been keeping the adoption a secret to "protect" the child, you may unconsciously reveal the child's adoption in a way that intensifies the sadness and the pain for the child, thus "proving" you were right to have kept this information from him.

Make arrangements with a therapist, social worker, or other individual familiar with adoption issues to see the child or your family shortly after you first talk with your child about his adoption. While you don't need to have the appointment scheduled ahead of time, have an individual selected and talk with that person ahead of time about what you will be doing and the need you will have to schedule an appointment on short notice once you find an opportunity to talk to your child.

Look for a natural opportunity to talk about your child's adoption, but don't wait too long to find one. Remember, you may have become adept at ignoring these natural opportunities. Because you didn't want to talk about adoption, you may have given your child the message that you were uncomfortable talking about certain things, so he may not ask questions that would easily lead to a discussion of his adoption. If a natural opportunity doesn't seem to present itself, you will have to initiate a discussion. In choosing a time to talk about this, make sure it's a time when you and your child are relaxed, when there is sufficient time to discuss the issues, and where the physical location is comfortable.

During your first discussion, remember that while the facts you are providing are important, it is also important to talk about feelings—yours and your child's—and to convey the attitude—verbally and nonverbally—that while you have been secretive in the past, you are willing now to talk about this issue or answer questions whenever your child chooses. This should be the first of many discussions.

You'll also want to explain why you thought you were keeping the secret, why you were really keeping the secret, and acknowledge that it was a mistake to keep the secret. Most likely, your child is not going to believe he benefited from the secret. He is more likely to think the secret was kept for your sake. If you're going to rebuild a relationship that has been damaged by deception, the best way to do it is by being honest. But keep in mind that you can explain mistakes in an empathetic way by incorporating the child's experiences into the explanation:

Parent: "When we decided to pretend you were daddy's biologic child as well as mine, we told ourselves that you would be better off not knowing. We couldn't tell you who your birthfather was. We knew with donor insemination that you'd never be able to find out. So, we thought, why tell you something that might only cause you to worry and wonder? The real reason, though, was that we were embarrassed to tell people that daddy was infertile and that mommy had to go to the doctor's office to conceive a baby.

Do you remember what it was like when you didn't know how to swim across the pool? You were embarrassed because other children your age could swim across the pool and when other children would ask you to go swimming with them, you made up a story about why you didn't want to go swimming because you were embarrassed that you couldn't do what other children your age could do. It was kind of like that for daddy and mommy.

But it was wrong for us to do that. And every time somebody said something like, "Michael's good-looking, like his dad," it would be harder to tell the truth. Have you ever told a lie, and then because of that lie, you had to tell more lies and finally you had told so many people so many lies that it got harder and harder to tell the truth even though you wanted to?"

While you'll want to fully explain how your child joined your family, he may not be able to absorb all the information.

Pay attention to signs that he has received as much information as he can handle *at this time* and end the discussion. You can say: "This is a lot of new information for you, and some new feelings, too. We can talk about this some more – when you want to and when I want to. But I think we ought to stop for now."

It may be a good idea to arrange for your child to have some vigorous physical activity after your discussion. Suggest a bike ride or a trip to the swimming pool or a run around the block. You have probably unleashed some intense emotions for him, and he may need to get rid of some of that tension physically. It's not a bad suggestion for you, either.

On the other hand, your child may want some private time for reflection.

Don't wait for your child to ask a question before having other conversations about his adoption. This has been a taboo subject for a long time. It may be hard for him to realize you're serious about wanting to discuss it openly. Continue to take the initiative to talk with your child about adoption. Be prepared to repeat information and clarify information as your child reframes his understanding of his history in light of this revelation. Many of the activities described earlier in this book can help children to organize their information about their birth families and their adoption experience and provide opportunities for parents and children to talk about adoption issues.

Don't wait for your child to show signs of psychological distress before having him talk about this new information with a counselor. While a child will not necessarily have psychological problems as a result of having a secret such as adoption revealed to him, he would probably benefit from discussing it with a therapist. Individual or family counseling is a way to prevent problems as well as to solve them.

Appendix A:
"Do We Need More Help?"

A mother I know was concerned because she had rebuffed her seven-year-old daughter's attempt to discuss adoption. They had been discussing adoption a lot in the family at that time, and when she tucked her daughter into bed one night, the girl asked if they could discuss something private. On that particular night, the girl had been using every ploy known to children to delay bedtime, and her mother instinctively believed her daughter's desire for private conversation was the latest try, so she said the discussion would have to wait. "It's about adoption," the daughter said. Her mother was reluctant to deny her daughter a chance to talk about adoption because she wanted her to know that she was always willing to talk about it. But she strongly suspected her daughter sensed this and was using it in her battle to stay up later. Her mother replied, "You know I'm always willing to discuss anything important to you, but it will have to wait until tomorrow because it's past your bedtime."

As parents, we have to be able to trust our instincts when communicating with our children. Some children are intensely interested in adoption and find it easy to talk about their concerns. Other children are less interested in adoption or are more reserved about sharing their thoughts and feelings. In discussing adoption, we need to make sure the subject is addressed whenever it is a legitimate issue, even if that means initiating a discussion ourselves or discussing adoption a lot at times. In some situations, initiating a discussion of adoption may help children verbalize their questions and concerns. On other occasions, it merely serves to let them know we understand and are available whenever they do want to talk.

Being sensitive to appropriate times to discuss adoption also means *not* bringing adoption into a situation in which it has no bearing, and *not* allowing our children to do that, either, just because we believe that openly discussing adoption is beneficial. If a discussion feels artificial, perhaps we are trying too hard. If we feel there is unfinished business that needs to be addressed, perhaps we aren't trying hard enough.

Normal childhood behavior

Sometimes children need more help dealing with being adopted than their parents feel capable of giving. More often, however, parents wonder whether their children's behavior is normal or requires professional intervention.

Becoming familiar with normal developmental behavior in children can help parents decide whether their child's behavior indicates a problem or is something to be expected (though not necessarily enjoyed). Talking with parents of nonadopted children can help adoptive parents understand normal childhood behavior, as can David Elkind's book *A Sympathetic Understanding of the Child: Birth to Sixteen* (Newton, Mass.: Allyn and Bacon, 1974) and books by the Gesell Institute of Human Development, including: *The Child from 5 to 10* by Arnold Gesell and Frances Ilg (New York: Harper & Row, 1977), and *Your Ten- to Fourteen-Year-Old*, by Louise Bates Ames, Frances L. Ilg, and Sidney M. Baker

(New York: Delacorte Press, 1988).

Listed below are some of the "normal" ways children behave at different ages, beginning with the ages at which an understanding of adoption begins to emerge. Of course, all children develop at different rates, and your child may not fit into these patterns exactly:

- Four-year-olds tend to be enthusiastic and energetic. However, they also have unreasonable fears, such as fear of dogs, birds, the dark, strange noises, and other common elements in their lives. They are also often fearful of monsters. Children this age generally believe that everything can be animated, including trees, toys, and rocks. They believe these objects can therefore have motives and intentions. They think it's possible for a plastic action figure to come alive in the toy closet and threaten them. Because they are exploring how people can be both good and bad, big and little, four-year-olds sometimes act immature or want to be bad.

- Five-year-olds tend to be calm and easy-going as they complete a major developmental period. Their fears are more temporary and concrete than the four-year-old's. They often intensify their attachment to their mother and fear their mothers will leave them or be gone when they awaken. The child who has bounded off to preschool for months without a backward glance suddenly cries, clings, and whines when it's time for mother to leave her. It isn't unusual for children this age to want their friends to come over and play rather than go to their friend's house.

- Age six is a time of transition, and the six-year-old is likely to be clumsy, less confident, and prone to emotional and physical extremes. Their move toward greater independence may be characterized by an increase in conflict with their mothers. They often react strongly to criticism. Children during the elementary school years worry about academic achievement and about being accepted by their peers.

• Seven-year-olds tend to be quiet and introspective as they digest all the new things they've been exposed to in the world, which is sometimes expressed as brooding. This is a time when they start to become modest about their bodies. More sensitive to others' reactions to them, they may complain that things are unfair or that others don't like them.

• Eight-year-olds tend to be more expansive, boisterous, outgoing, and self-confident. They embrace the world by charging into it. This is the age at which a child is likely to break his arm by falling out of a tree. They are curious and enjoy discovery. They discover their parents (and others) are not perfect and develop a judgmental attitude.

• Nine-year-olds are more mature eight-year-olds. They have more self-control and are more self-motivated. They are more accepting of parental mistakes and are better able to accept responsibility for their actions. However, they sometimes project a "know-it-all" attitude.

• Age ten is a time of equilibrium or balance, again due to the completion of a major developmental period. The angry and sad feelings of ten-year-olds tend to be resolved quickly. They are comfortable with themselves and their families. You may find yourself feeling more confident leaving a ten-year-old home alone than an eleven- or twelve-year-old.

• Eleven-year-olds are confrontational – even quarrelsome, resistant to suggestions, and defiant of parental authority. Their emotions are also in upheaval. They are not sure what to do with their angry or sad feelings, and often dissolve into tears. Energetic eleven-year-olds want to be where the action is, but are also somewhat concerned about being alone. When alone, they fear burglars, kidnappers, and other unseen menaces. While eleven-year-olds have a hard time getting along with parents and siblings, they are often pleasant with those outside the family. Cooperation away from home can be a good sign that their confrontational behavior at home is normal.

• Twelve-year-olds usually give their families a bit of a reprieve. They are more outgoing, enthusiastic, and generous than they were at eleven. This is not to imply that living with a twelve-year-old is easy. They still have strong emotions and strong emotional swings, but they aren't as tearful or as quarrelsome as they have been. And they display extremes of dependence and independence. While they are still critical of themselves and their parents, they find more socially acceptable ways of expressing that criticism than they did the previous year.

• Thirteen-year-olds tend to be inactive physically but active intellectually and emotionally. This is a year of introspection and preoccupation with self, which often leads to unhappiness with self and sensitivity to real or perceived insults. Thirteen-year-olds are argumentative and want to protect their thoughts and feelings. Attempts to get them to confide their thoughts and feelings may be seen as prying. They are very much trying to understand themselves.

• Fourteen-year-olds have worked through some of the anxieties that were so troubling at thirteen and are more outgoing and less moody. But there are still conflicts with parents and siblings. In particular, fourteen-year-olds may be more critical of their fathers than they have been in the past, when most of their criticism was reserved for their mothers.

• Fifteen-year-olds are again quiet, reflective, and guarded about themselves. They tend to withdraw physically from the family. They are beginning to recognize the responsibilities of adulthood and independence and are on the verge of being able to realistically assess themselves and the world. This is all very sobering, and takes a lot of thinking, as well. Adults may represent not only an intrusion but a reminder that the adolescent is still as close to childhood as he is to adulthood.

The Gesell Institute of Human Development recommends

that parents deal with fifteen-year-olds by respecting their intellectual abilities and encouraging them to use them, feigning disinterest so that they don't think the parent is prying, and allowing them just a little bit more freedom than the parent is sure they can handle.

• Around the age of sixteen, adolescents seem to pull themselves together. They are comfortable with who they are, so they don't feel the need to protect themselves as actively. Nor do they care as much about what others think of them. They respond rather than react. They are less sensitive and less moody. In general, they are easier to live with.

Grieving

Children, including infants and toddlers, grieve when they experience a loss. If your child comes into your family after having formed an attachment to a caretaker, she is likely to experience the stages of grief described in Chapter 4. Even an infant unable to recognize her caretaker notices the disruption in her schedule or differences in smells and sounds, and may show signs of grief as a result.

As discussed in Chapters 4 and 6, children may also grieve many years after their adoption, when they understand that they have lost significant people in their lives.

Although grieving for a loss is normal, if a child does not seem to be able to move smoothly through the stages of grief, parents may want to seek professional help for their child.

Claudia Jewett's book *Helping Children Cope with Separation and Loss* (Harvard, Mass.: Harvard Common Press, 1982), describes how children grieve and how parents can help them when they are grieving.

Recognizing when children need help

Some children will need professional counseling to deal

with adoption issues. Signs that a child is having problems requiring therapy include, but are not limited to: an inability to proceed through the stages of grief, psychosomatic physical complaints, problems with concentration, poor reports from school, aggressive behavior, inappropriate sexual behavior, difficulty relating to others, a particular nightmare that recurs repeatedly or head-banging during sleep, bedwetting and other elimination problems, setting fires, harming animals, excessive withdrawal, compulsive behavior (including trying to be perfect or overachieving), eating disorders, comments about suicide or suicide attempts, drug or alcohol abuse, or any other behavior that a parent or other adult is concerned about.

If you (or a teacher or other concerned adult) think your child is having problems, don't hesitate to seek help. Even if you are not sure that the problem is related to adoption, choose a therapist or counselor sensitive to adoption issues so that possibility can be explored. (See "Where to go for more information," below.) If none are available in your community, provide the counselor or therapist you choose with a copy of *Clinical Practice in Adoption,* by Robin C. Winkler, Dirck W. Brown, Margaret van Keppel, and Amy Blanchard (New York: Pergamon Press, 1988). It's a succinct guide to the major issues for those adopted traditionally or through donor insemination and surrogacy. (If your therapist isn't receptive to being given educational materials, find another therapist.)

Where to go for more information

Established by Congress and opened in 1988, the **National Adoption Information Clearinghouse**, Suite 600, 1400 Eye St. N.W., Washington, D.C. 20005, (202) 842-1919, collects and disseminates information about all aspects of adoption. Individuals interested in finding a therapist specializing in adoption, an adoption consultant, or public speaker on adoption issues can contact the clearinghouse for referrals. The clearinghouse also publishes an annual directory of adoption agencies and adoptive parent support groups, a directory of crisis pregnancy shelters and counseling centers, and a list of audiovisual materials on adoption. Abstracts of articles and books about adoption are available through its database.

Adoptive parent groups

Many communities, including small ones, have active adoptive parent groups that can provide support, education, and referral. Because the addresses and phone numbers for these groups often change with every change in leadership, the quickest way to find them is often through telephone calls to your local adoption agencies. The following national organizations can also refer you to their member groups:

Adoptive Families of America (formerly **OURS, Inc.**), 3307 Highway 100 North, Suite 203, Minneapolis, Minn. 55422, (612) 434-4930.

Adoptive Families of America is rapidly growing from an umbrella organization for local parent support groups with emphasis on intercountry and special needs adoption to more of a leadership role in the adoption community. They are the best single source of multi-cultural materials for foreign-born adoptees, and operate a 24-hour helpline. Write to them for information about magazines they publish and books they sell.

North American Council on Adoptable Children (NACAC), 1821 University Ave., Suite S-275, St. Paul, Minn. 55104, (612) 644-3036.

NACAC is a strong advocate for special needs adoptions, both by providing education and support for individuals and agencies, and through lobbying efforts. NACAC has a representative in each state who maintains lists of adoptive parent groups and other resources.

Resolve, Inc., 5 Water St., Arlington, Mass. 02174, (617) 643-2424.

Resolve, Inc., primarily provides education and support about infertility, but because many of its members have adopted, both the national headquarters and local chapters are excellent resources for adoptive parents.

Services to adoptive families

Some adoption agencies are more active than others in providing adoptive parents with what is called "post-placement services," that is, help with issues and situations that arise after the adoption is completed. Local adoptive parent organizations can refer parents to those local agencies with active post-placement programs. Most of these do not restrict their services to parents who adopted through them.

An increasing number of knowledgeable individuals and trained therapists also offer educational and consulting services on adoption. Contact the National Adoption Information Clearinghouse (above) for referrals, or inquire at a local adoption agency or adoptive parent organization.

Many adoption organizations and adoptive parent groups sponsor one-day conferences on adoption, often featuring a nationally known speaker. In addition to the other benefits they receive from belonging to an adoptive parents' organization, members are notified of local and national conferences.

Other resources

There are many other excellent resources for adoptive parents. The following are particularly helpful:

Donors' Offspring, P.O. Box 33, Sarcoxie, Mo. 64862, (417) 548-3679.

One of the few sources of education and support for those adopted through donor insemination and reproductive technology.

Parenting Resources, 250 El Camino Real, Suite 111, Tustin, Calif. 92680, (714) 669-8100.

Provides education, counseling, and mediation services to adoptive and birth families.

Raising Adopted Children, by Lois Ruskai Melina (New York: Harper & Row, 1986).

A comprehensive discussion of issues and situations that are likely to arise in adoptive families from the time of placement, including the adjustment of parents and children, bonding and attachment, and the psychological impact of adoption and infertility.

Adopted Child. P.O. Box 9362, Moscow, Id. 83843, (208) 882-1181.

A four-page monthly newsletter edited by Lois Ruskai Melina that provides information and advice on raising adopted children, reports of research, and book reviews.

The Adoption Resource Book, rev. ed. by Lois Gilman (New York: Harper & Row, 1987).

Although primarily directed at prospective adoptive parents, the resource lists in this book are beneficial to those who have adopted, as well.

Lost & Found: The Adoption Experience, rev. ed. by Betty Jean Lifton (New York: Harper & Row, 1988).

Contains a comprehensive list of adoption consultants and organizations, particularly those involved in search and reunion.

Having Your Baby by Donor Insemination, by Elizabeth Noble (Boston: Houghton Mifflin, 1987).

Primarily a guide for those considering donor insemination, advocates being honest with children adopted through donor insemination and contains an extensive resource guide.

Lethal Secrets: The Shocking Consequences and Unsolved Problems of Artificial Insemination, by Annette Baran and Reuben Pannor (New York: Warner Books, 1989).

Discussion of the effect of donor insemination on families, by the authors of the classic and insightful book, *The Adoption Triangle* (see the Activity section at the end of Chapter 7 for a complete reference).

Appendix B:
Bibliography of Children's Books

Most of the children's literature dealing with adoption and foster care is fictional. However, many of the fictional stories are not as realistic as they could be. In real life, the conflict, suspense, and emotions of children in the child welfare system are often too dramatic for children to read about. Though unrealistic, these stories should not be ignored, for they accurately depict children's feelings of anger, rejection, and suspicion, as well as their need for love and a permanent family. Furthermore, they may be more interesting for a child to read (or for a parent to read to a child) than a nonfiction book.

Not every book about adoption is listed here. Some books are out of date; others do not convey positive attitudes toward birthparents or adoption; and some were unavailable for review at the time this book was written. And more books for children about adoption are published each year, making any list that attempts to be comprehensive immediately out-of-date. But this list of ninety children's books about adoption and foster care provides a variety of entertaining and educational choices.

The books have been listed by age group, but this is only a guide. Some younger children will be ready for books geared to slightly older readers, while some older children still enjoy picture books. Most of these books are available through libraries, but the addresses of publishers that might be unfamiliar to readers are included.

Following this bibliography is an index that will direct readers to books about particular topics in adoption and foster care.

Preschool-Kindergarten
Nonfiction

1. *How Babies and Families are Made (There is more than one way!)*, by Patricia Schaffer. (Tabor Sarah Books, 2419 Jefferson Ave., Berkeley, Calif. 94703, 1988).
   Well-done book that covers all types of reproduction and birth, including donor insemination, *in vitro* fertilization, twins, miscarriage, premature birth, and cesarean section. It also explains that after birth, some children are adopted.

2. *How I Began: The Story of Donor Insemination*, by Julia Paul, ed. (Fertility Society of Australia, Care Reproductive Biology Unit, The Royal Women's Hospital, 132 Grattan St., Carlton, Victoria, 3053, Australia, 1988).
   Describes donor insemination simply and accurately.

3. *Our Baby: A Birth and Adoption Story*, by Janice Koch. (Perspectives Press, P.O. Box 90318, Indianapolis, Ind. 46290-0318, 1985).
   Explains how babies are conceived and born, and how some are then adopted.

4. *Why Was I Adopted?* by Carole Livingston. (Secaucus, N.J.: Lyle Stuart, 1978).
   One of the most popular books for children about adoption, this book presents the motives of adoptive parents and the reasons children become available for adoption.

Fiction

5. *The Chosen Baby*, by Valentina P. Wasson. (New York: J.B. Lippincott Co., 1977).
   This book retains its original title, reflecting adoption thought in 1939, but has been updated to describe the process of adopting an infant today.

6. *Do I Have a Daddy?* by Jeanne Warren Lindsay. (Morning Glory Press, 6595 San Haroldo Way, Buena Park, Calif. 90620, 1982).
   A single parent explains to her son why she never married his father, and why his father has no contact with him.

7. *The Foundling Fox*, by Irina Korschunow. (New York: Harper & Row, 1984).
   A delightful story of a mother fox who finds a fox kit and comes to love it as one of her own. The reaction of the fox's neighbors to her adoption is particularly enjoyable.

8. *I Am Adopted*, by Susan Lapsley. (London: The Bodley Head, 1974, Distributed in the United States by Merrimack Book Service, 250 Commercial St., Manchester, N.H. 03101).
   A simple picture book that conveys the idea that adoption means belonging to a family.

9. *I Wish I Had My Father*, by Norma Simon. (Albert Whitman & Co., 5747 W. Howard St., Niles, Ill. 60648, 1983).
   A boy who has not had contact with his father since his parents' divorce expresses his sad and angry feelings about Father's Day.

10. *Jane Is Adopted*, by Althea. (London: Souvenir Press, 1980, Contact Bookstall Services, 86 Abbey St., Derby, England DE3 3SQ for this and other titles from British publishers).
    Explains adoption as a way of belonging to a family.

11. *Katie-Bo: An Adoption Story*, by Iris L. Fisher. (Adama Books, 306 W. 38th St., New York, N.Y. 10018, 1987). Warm and humorous story of the adoption of a Korean baby from the viewpoint of an older child in the family.

12. *Miss Suzy's Birthday*, by Miriam Young. (Parents' Magazine Press, 685 Third Ave., New York, N.Y. 10017, 1974). Pleasant story of four adopted squirrels who plan a birthday party for their mother.

13. *My Little Foster Sister*, by Muriel Stanek. (Albert Whitman & Co., 5747 W. Howard St., Niles, Ill. 60648, 1981).
Sensitively describes the jealousy a child in a family might feel when a foster child comes to live with the family, although the foster child's situation is not realistic.

14. *My Name is Mike Trumsky*, by Ruth Piepgras. (The Child's World, 980 N. McLean Blvd., Elgin, Ill. 60123, 1979).
A foster child is confused about relationships in his new family and wonders why he hasn't heard from his birthmother.

15. *Susan and Gordon Adopt a Baby,* based on the Sesame Street Television scripts by Judy Freudberg and Tony Geiss. (New York: Random House/Children's Television Workshop, 1986).
Big Bird feels left out when the new baby adopted by Susan and Gordon receives all the attention.

Early Elementary School
Nonfiction

16. *Being Adopted*, by Maxine B. Rosenberg. (New York: Lathrop, Lee & Shepard Books, 1984).
Profiles three adoptees who are racially or culturally different from their families.

17. *Is That Your Sister?*, by Catherine Bunin and Sherry Bunin. (New York: Pantheon Books, 1976).
    A six-year-old adoptee gives her perspective on transracial adoption.

18. *We Don't Look Like Our Mom and Dad*, by Harriet Langsam Sobol. (New York: Coward-McCann, 1984).
    A photo-essay of the Levin family, which includes two Asian-American adoptees.

Fiction

19. *Aaron's Door*, by Miska Miles. (Boston: Little, Brown & Co., 1977).
    An older child has ambivalent feelings about adoption during his first few days in his adoptive family.

20. *Adoption Is for Always*, by Linda Walvoord Girard. (Albert Whitman & Co., 5747 W. Howard St., Niles, Ill. 60648, 1986).
    A young girl is hurt and angry when she first understands that being adopted means she has birth-parents who didn't keep her.

21. *The Boy Who Wanted a Family*, by Shirley Gordon. (New York: Harper & Row, 1980).
    Based on the author's personal experience, this book describes the year after placement and before finalization for a seven-year-old boy adopted by a single mother.

22. *Brothers Are All the Same*, by Mary Milgram. (New York: E.P. Dutton & Co., 1978).
    Siblings react to the charge by a neighbor boy that an adoptive brother is not a 'real' brother.

23. *Families Grow in Different Ways*, by Barbara Parrish-Benson. (Waterloo, Ont.: Before We Are Six, 1973).
    Two friends wait for babies to join their families – one by birth and one by adoption.

24. *The Hollywell Family*, by Margaret Kornitzer. (London: The Bodley Head, 1973).
Describes the adoption of an African-English baby by a family with one biologic child.

25. *Just Momma and Me*, by Christine Engla Eber. (Lollipop Power, Inc., P.O. Box 277, Carrboro, N.C. 27510, 1975).
An unusual story about the feelings of jealousy a girl adopted by a single mother has when her mother's boyfriend moves in, and later, when her mother becomes pregnant.

26. *Lyle Finds His Mother*, by Bernard Waber. (Boston: Houghton Mifflin Co., 1974).
Lyle, a crocodile who lives with a human family, becomes curious about his mother and searches for her, finding obvious similarities.

27. *The Mulberry Bird*, by Anne Braff Brodzinsky. (Perspectives Press, P.O. Box 90318, Indianapolis, Ind. 46290-0318, 1986).
A mulberry bird is unable to properly care for her baby bird despite her desire to, so a wise owl sees that the baby bird finds a home with shore birds.

28. *A Quiet Place*, by Rose Blue. (Franklin Watts, 387 Paul Avenue South, New York, N.Y. 10016, 1969).
A nine-year-old foster boy must search for a place where he can go for privacy when his favorite haunt, the library, closes for renovation.

29. *Somebody Else's Child*, by Roberta Silman. (Frederick Warne & Co., 40 W. 23rd St., New York, N.Y. 10010, 1976).
A fourth grader is hurt when an adult friend misunderstands adoptive relationships.

30. *Twice Upon-A-Time: Born and Adopted*, by Eleanora Patterson. (EP Press, P.O. Box 6262, Brattleboro, Vt. 05301, 1987).

Although the text is somewhat awkward at times, this book contains wonderful illustrations and provides a simple look at adoption issues from conception to questions a child may have about birthparents.

Late Elementary School
Nonfiction

31. *Do You Have Your Father's Nose?* by Julian May. (Creative Educational Society, P.O. Box 227, Mankato, Minn. 56001, 1970).
Simple but clear explanation of heredity.

32. *How It Feels To Be Adopted*, by Jill Krementz. (New York: Alfred A. Knopf, 1982).
Nineteen children ages eight to sixteen describe their feelings about being adopted.

33. *Mine for a Year*, by Susan Kuklin. (New York: Coward-McCann, Inc., 1984).
The touching, true story of a foster boy who raises a puppy for a year before it is sent to be trained as a seeing eye dog. The parallels between the boy's experience loving and caring for a dog that he knows is only with him temporarily, and his own experience as a foster son, are evident, but not overtly made.

34. *Welcome Child*, by Pearl S. Buck. (New York: The John Day Co., 1963).
Although the photographs in this book are dated, as is some of the explanation of adoption, this is a warm story of the first few months in the life of a young girl from Korea who is adopted by a couple in the United States.

Fiction

35. *And I'm Stuck With Joseph*, by Susan Sommer. (Herald Press, 616 Walnut Ave., Scottdale, Penn. 15683, 1984).
An eleven-year-old is frustrated by her new brother's

behavior when her parents adopt a three-year-old.

36. *Barney and the UFO*, by Margaret Goff Clark. (New York: Dodd, Mead & Co., 1979).
    A foster boy, who wants to be adopted but resists forming an attachment to his foster parents in case they do not adopt him, finds that his love for his foster parents is the only thing that saves him from being abducted by an alien, in a story that is more allegory than science fiction.

37. *Bugs in Your Ears*, by Betty Bates. (Holiday House, 18 E. 53rd St., New York, N.Y. 10022, 1977).
    An eighth grade girl struggles with her feelings about her birthfather, an alcoholic, when her stepfather wants to adopt her.

38. *The Cat That Was Left Behind*, by C. S. Adler. (New York: Clarion Books, 1981).
    A thirteen-year-old boy learns to accept that his birthmother had made an adoption plan for him and accepts his foster family as his adoptive family.

39. *A December Tale*, by Marilyn Sachs. (Garden City, N.Y.: Doubleday, 1976).
    The helpless and hopeless feelings of a ten-year-old girl in a foster family clearly come through as she escapes from her abusive situation through fantasies of conversations with Joan of Arc. The ending of this story, in which the girl and her brother run away from the foster family, seems to offer false hope, but the insight into the effects of psychological and physical abuse is good.

40. *Edgar Allen*, by John Neufeld. (S. G. Phillips, P.O. Box 83, Chatham, N.Y. 12037, 1968).
    This story, which was published at the peak of the civil rights movement, seems a bit dated as it describes the reaction of a conservative community to a family's plan to adopt an African–American baby. However, it presents honestly the feelings of the other children in

the family when the parents disrupt the adoption in the face of community pressure.

41. *Elizabeth Gail and the Mystery at the Johnson Farm*, by Hilda Stahl. (Tyndale House, P.O. Box 80, Wheaton, Ill. 60189, 1978).

    Christian themes dominate this book about parents who believe their new foster daughter is responsible for a series of disturbing events, but eventually learn the truth. The first in a series of books about Elizabeth Gail.

42. *A Family Apart*, by Joan Lowery Nixon. (New York: Bantam Books, 1987).

    The first in a series of historical novels about the orphan trains that took children from the East to the Midwest for adoption during the nineteenth century.

43. *Foster Child*, by Marion Dane Bauer. (New York: Seabury Press, 1977).

    This at first appears to be a familiar story of a foster child who learns to accept the reality that she would never be 'rescued' by her birthparent. However, the main character in the story is sexually abused by her foster father, a religious zealot, and the book does an excellent job of presenting her feelings of revulsion as well as her vulnerability to someone who appears to offer physical affection. As with most books about complicated topics for children this age, the happy ending is a bit contrived.

44. *Foster Mary*, by Celia Strang. (New York: McGraw-Hill, 1979).

    A family of apple pickers, formed through the informal adoption of the children of migrant workers, struggle to make a permanent home in Washington.

45. *Fox Farm*, by Eileen Dunlop. (New York: Holt, Rinehart and Winston, 1978).

    A ten-year-old boy works through his feelings of rejection as he befriends an abandoned pup while living with a foster family.

46. *Grandmother Orphan,* by Phyllis Green. (Thomas Nelson, P.O. Box 141000, Nashville, Tenn. 37214, 1977).

   An adoptee sent to visit her grandmother after the girl is caught shoplifting confronts her own feelings after learning her adoptive mother was adopted and her adoptive grandmother grew up in an orphanage.

47. *The Great Gilly Hopkins,* by Katherine Paterson. (New York: Avon Books, 1978).

   An intelligent but troublesome girl forms an attachment to her foster family despite her efforts to remain aloof, and discovers that her birthmother is not as she imagined her to be. This is an interesting story with an ending that is upbeat without being overly romantic.

48. *I, Rebekah, Take You, the Lawrences,* by Julia First. (Franklin Watts, 387 Park Ave. South, New York, N.Y. 10016, 1981).

   A twelve-year-old girl describes her feelings as she is adopted. The story is somewhat sugar-coated, but there is good insight into the feelings the girl has as she waits to be adopted, feels guilty at being adopted when some of her friends are not, and fears becoming attached to new parents.

49. *It Must've Been the Fish Sticks,* by Betty Bates. (New York: Holiday House, 18 E. 53rd St., New York, N.Y. 10022, 1982).

   When an eighth-grade boy, adopted by his stepmother, learns his biologic mother is not dead, as he had assumed, he goes to visit her. While parents might wish some of the issues had been more fully explored, the story does show what it is like when an adolescent meets a birthparent whose values are different from those he grew up with.

50. *It's Me, Christy,* by Phyllis Green. (Scholastic Book Services, 730 Broadway, New York, N.Y. 10003, 1977). See *Grandmother Orphan.*

51. *Karen's Sister*, by Elisabet McHugh. (New York: Green-willow Books, 1983).

    In the sequel to *Raising a Mother Isn't Easy*, a single mother's decision to adopt a five-year-old girl from Korea and marry a widower with three children is seen through the mature eyes of her eleven-year-old daughter, who is also adopted and also from Korea.

52. *Matthew, Mark, Luke and John*, by Pearl S. Buck. (New York: John Day Company, 1966).

    A glimpse of what life was like for Amerasian children in post-war Korea, in a story that ends happily.

53. *Miracle of Time: Adoptng a Sister*, by Jane Claypool Miner. (Crestwood House, P.O. Box 3427, Mankato, Minn. 56002, 1982).

    A girl must deal with her unfulfilled fantasies when her parents adopt a severely traumatized five-year-old Vietnamese orphan.

54. *The Pinballs*, by Betsy Byars. (New York: Harper & Row, 1977).

    Three children – a teenage boy and girl, and an eight-year-old boy – confront feelings of loss and rejection when they are placed with the same foster parents, and learn that they can make choices about their own lives.

55. *Raising a Mother Isn't Easy*, by Elisabet McHugh. (New York: Greenwillow Books, 1983).

    A Korean girl adopted by a single mother tries to find a husband for her mother.

56. *Second-hand Family*, by Richard Parker. (Indianapolis: Bobbs-Merrill Co., Inc., 1965).

    Peculiar story about a boy adopted into an odd foster family.

57. *Seven Years From Home*, by Rose Blue. (Raintree Publishers, 310 W. Wisconsin, Mezzanine Level, Milwaukee, Wisc. 53203, 1976).

    Depicts the emotional struggles of an eleven-year-old

boy who is adopted, including his curiosity about his biologic parents, his anger at being adopted, and his jealousy of his brother who was born into the family.

58. *Silent Fear*, by Nancy Smiler Levinson. (Crestwood House, P.O. Box 3427, Mankato, Minn. 56002, 1981).
A girl is physically abused by her foster mother, but finds help when she confides in a friend and a teacher.

59. *Star Island Boy*, by Louise Dickinson Rich. (Franklin Watts, 387 Park Ave. South, New York, N.Y. 10016, 1968).
A twelve-year-old boy who has been in foster families all his life finds a permanent home.

60. *Tell Me No Lies*, by Hila Colman. (New York: Crown Publishers, Inc., 1978).
When her new stepfather wants to adopt her, a thirteen-year-old girl learns that her mother was never married to her biologic father and never told him about her pregnancy. After meeting her birthfather, the girl learns an important lesson about life.

61. *Tina Gogo*, by Judie Angell. (Bradbury Press, 866 Third Ave., New York, N.Y. 10022, 1978).
An eleven-year-old girl becomes friends with an angry girl who doesn't admit that she is a foster child.

62. *Toby Lived Here*, by Hilma Wolitzer. (New York: Farrar, Straus, Giroux, 1978).
Feelings of embarrassment, loss, and loyalty are explored in this story of two sisters who are temporarily placed in a foster family during their mother's hospitalization for mental illness.

63. *Visiting Miss Pierce*, by Pat Derby. (New York: Farrar, Straus, Giroux, 1986).
A fourteen-year-old boy confronts his own feelings about being adopted when he makes friends with an elderly woman and learns that her younger brother once placed a baby for adoption.

64. *Where the River Begins*, by Patricia M. St. John. (Moody Press, 820 N. LaSalle Dr., Chicago, Ill. 60610, 1980).
   A boy who is emotionally abused by his mother and stepfather finds guidance and love in a Christian foster family.

65. *Without Hats, Who Can Tell the Good Guys?* by Mildred Ames. (New York: E. P. Dutton, 1976).
   A boy disappoints his foster father by not being a good baseball player, but eventually is accepted for himself and accepts his foster family.

66. *Won't Know Till I Get There*, by Walter Dean Myers. (New York: Viking Press, 1982).
   A fourteen-year-old boy describes the adoption of a thirteen-year-old with a criminal record in an often amusing story.

67. *Yes, My Darling Daughter*, by Evelyn Swetnam. (New York: Harvey House, 1978).
   An eleven-year-old foster girl learns to trust—and love—her foster parents.

Junior High and Up
Nonfiction

68. *Adoption*, by Elaine Scott. (New York: Franklin Watts, 387 Park Ave. South, New York, N.Y. 10016, 1980).
   Discussions of the adoption process, feelings adoptees have about being adopted, heredity and environment, and options for pregnant women are included in this book.

69. *Adoption: The Facts, Feelings and Issues of a Double Heritage*, by Jeanne DuPrau. (Julian Messner, Prentice Hall Bldg., Route 9W, Englewood Cliffs, N.J. 07632, 1981).
   Perhaps more suitable for nonadopted adolescents, this book describes adoption in a simple and emotionally detached way.

70. *Foster Care and Adoption*, by Margaret O. Hyde. (Franklin Watts, 387 Park Ave. South, New York, N.Y. 10016, 1982).

This book describes adoption and foster care, including surrogacy, open adoptions, and searching for biologic relatives.

71. *So You're Adopted*, by Fred Powledge. (New York: Charles Scribner's Sons, 1982).

The author's own experience as an adoptee gives authenticity to his answers to questions teenagers have about adoption, such as whether it is normal to not be curious about one's birthparents and how to talk to one's adoptive parents about adoption.

72. *Test-Tube Life*, by Gerald S. Snyder. (Julian Messner, Prentice Hall Bldg., Route 9W, Englewood Cliffs, N.J. 07632, 1982).

Describes the scientific advances in reproductive technology and the ethical questions raised by the new technology. However, it seems to support not telling children they were conceived by donor insemination.

Fiction

73. *About David*, by Susan Beth Pfeffer. (New York: Delacorte Press, 1980).

A girl struggles with her feelings when a long-time friend murders his adoptive parents and then kills himself. Presents the adoptee as an individual with adoption issues and emotional problems rather than suggesting all adoptees are troubled.

74. *The Adoption Experience*, by Steven Nickman. (Julian Messner, Prentice Hall Bldg., Route 9W, Englewood Cliffs, N.J. 07632, 1985).

Seven fictional stories explore different aspects of adoption, with each followed by a commentary by the author—a pediatrician and psychiatrist.

75. *Bones on Black Spruce Mountain*, by David Budbill. (New York: Dial Press, 1978).

    A teenager adopted at the age of eight confronts his feelings about his past while investigating a local legend about a child who died after running away from abusive foster parents.

76. *Brothers by Choice*, by Elfreida Read. (New York: Farrar, Straus, Giroux, 1974).

    An adolescent runs away from home because he doesn't believe he is living up to his adoptive father's expectations, but learns something about love and commitment through his adoptive brother's attempt to bring him home.

77. *The Disappearance*, by Rosa Guy. (London: Victor Gollancz, Ltd., 1984).

    When a little girl disappears from her home two days after her family takes a street-wise teenager from Harlem as a foster son, the boy becomes the prime suspect. This is a serious book with mature themes.

78. Find a Stranger, Say Good-bye, by Lois Lowry. (New York: Pocket Books, 1978).

    A high school graduate searches for her biologic mother.

79. *I'm Still Me*, by Betty Jean Lifton. (New York: Bantam Books, 1986).

    An adolescent searches for and finds her birthmother.

80. *The Iron Doors Between*, by James L. Summers. (Westminster Press, P.O. Box 718, William Penn Annex, Philadelphia, Pa. 19105, 1968).

    Realistic portrayal of a boy whose adoptive family is disrupted by mental illness, and who subsequently gets into trouble with the law. Out on parole, his foster parents, teachers, and friends struggle to help him, but he is drawn to less desirable friends with inevitable consequences.

81. *Kate's Story*, by Christopher Leach. (Four Winds Press, P.O. Box 548, Village Station, New York, N.Y. 10014, 1968).

   Interesting story of a girl who discovers at the age of nine that she is adopted. As she goes through adolescence, she fantasizes about her biologic parents, and her relationship with her adoptive mother is strained.

82. *Kim/Kimi*, by Hadley Irwin. (New York: Margaret K. McElderry Books, 1987).

   Although she loves her mother, stepfather, and stepbrother, a teenage girl feels compelled to learn something about her Japanese-American father, who died before she was born, and her ethnic heritage.

83. *Mad Martin*, by Patricia Windsor. (New York: Harper & Row, 1976).

   Excellent story about a boy who is emotionally neglected and consequently cannot recognize his own feelings until he is placed in a foster family. While the ending is unrealistic, the book provides insight into the world of the depressed child.

84. *Mother, How Could You!* by Eve Bunting. (New York: Pocket Books, 1984).

   Well-done story about a teenager's reaction to her mother's plan to become a surrogate mother.

85. *Nothing but a Stranger*, by Arlene Hale. (Four Winds Press, P.O. Box 548, Village Station, New York, N.Y. 10014, 1966).

   An eighteen-year-old girl discovers she is adopted, finds her birthfather, and comes to understand her relationships with members of her adoptive family.

86. *The Secret Lover of Elmtree*, by Arthur J. Roth. (Four Winds Press, P.O. Box 548, Village Station, New York, N.Y. 10014, 1976).

   A teenage boy who is adopted is found by his birthfather who offers him opportunities his adoptive family cannot, creating stress that eventually leads to a suicide attempt.

87. *The Sound of Coaches*, by Leon Garfield. (New York: Viking Press, 1974).
Set in eighteenth century England, this story describes an adopted boy's relationship with his adoptive parents, his fantasies about his birthfather, and the effect on himself and his adoptive parents when he encounters his birthfather by chance. An unusual story in that it focuses on the child's interest in his birthfather.

88. *Vicky*, by Catherine Storr. (London: Faber and Faber, 1981).
After her adoptive mother dies, sixteen-year-old Vicky decides to search for information about her biologic parents, even though she knows her biologic mother is dead. Although the search goes more easily than is generally the case, this book is more realistic than most in showing the conflicting emotions of the adopted teenager and her adoptive family.

89. *Which Mother Is Mine?* by Joan L. Oppenheimer. (New York: Bantam Books, 1980).
A teenager has conflicting emotions when she faces the possibility of leaving the foster family she has lived with for six years and who wants to adopt her or returning to her birthmother to live.

90. *Who Is David?: A Story of an Adopted Adolescent and His Friends*, by Evelyn Nerlove. (Child Welfare League of America, 440 First St. N.W., Suite 310, Washington D.C. 20001, 1985).
The beneficial effect of adoption groups for adolescents and their families becomes clear in this story.

Index to Bibliography
of Children's Books

Sources

Ames, Louise Bates, Frances L. Ilg, and Sidney M. Baker. *Your Ten- to Fourteen-Year-Old.* New York: Delacorte Press, 1988.

Brodzinsky, David M., Leslie M. Singer, and Anne M. Braff. "Children's Understanding of Adoption." *Child Development* 55 (June 1984): 869-878.

Elkind, David. *All Grown Up & No Place to Go: Teenagers in Crisis.* Reading, Mass.: Addison-Wesley, 1984.

__. *Child Development and Education: A Piagetian Perspective.* New York: Oxford University Press, 1976.

__. *A Sympathetic Understanding of the Child: Birth to Sixteen.* Newton, Mass: Allyn and Bacon, 1974.

__. *Children and Adolescents: Interpretive Essays on Jean Piaget.* 3d ed. New York: Oxford University Press, 1981.

Erikson, Erik H. *Childhood and Society.* 2d ed. New York: W.W. Norton & Co., 1964.

__. *Identity, Youth, and Crisis.* New York: W.W. Norton & Co., 1968.

Fahlberg, Vera. *Child Development*. N.p.: Michigan Department of Social Services, 1982.

Gesell, Arnold, and Frances Ilg. *The Child from 5 to 10*. New York: Harper & Row, 1977.

Jewett, Claudia L. *Helping Children Cope with Separation and Loss*. Harvard, Mass.: Harvard Common Press, 1982.

Manaster, Guy J. *Adolescent Development and the Life Tasks*. Boston: Allyn and Bacon, 1977.

McDonald, Marjorie. *Not By the Color of their Skin: The Impact of Racial Differences on the Child's Development*. N.p., International University Press, 1970.

Milner, David. *Children and Race*. Beverly Hills, Calif.: SAGE Publications, 1983.

Pannor, Reuben, and Evelyn A. Nerlove. "Fostering Understanding Between Adolescents and Adoptive Parents Through Group Experiences." *Child Welfare* 56 (September–October 1977): 537-545.

Piaget, Jean, and Barbel Inhelder. *The Psychology of the Child*. New York: Basic Books, 1969.

Porter, Judith D.R. *Black Child, White Child*. Cambridge, Mass.: Harvard University Press, 1971.

Powell, Azizi. "Raise Your Child with Ethnic Pride." *OURS Magazine*. (November-December 1988): 26-29.

Schaffer, Patricia. *How Babies and Families are Made: There is more than one way!)*. Berkeley, Calif.: Tabor Sarah Books, 1988.

Snowden, R., and G.D. Mitchell. *The Artificial Family: A Consideration of Artificial Insemination by Donor*. London: Allen & Unwin, 1981.

Sorosky, Arthur D., Annette Baran, and Reuben Pannor. *The Adoption Triangle: The Effects of the Sealed Record on Adoptees, Birth Parents, and Adoptive Parents.* Garden City, N.Y.: Anchor Books, 1979.

Williams, John E., and J. Kenneth Morland. *Race, Color, and the Young Child.* Chapel Hill, N.C.: University of North Carolina Press, 1976.

Index

Nerlove, Evelyn, 206
Noble, Elizabeth, 24, 227, 246
North American Council on Adoptable Children (NACAC), 244–245
Nurturing Today, 4

older child adoption (see adoption, of older children)
open adoption (see adoption, open)

Pannor, Reuben, 94, 201, 225, 227, 247
Parenting Resources, 246
Powell, Azizi, 70, 153
preschoolers, 3, 53–66, 239
    feelings about adoption, 62–63
    play and, 64–66
    magical thinking, 65–66
    racial awareness of, 46, 66–72
    relationship with extended family, 72–78
    understanding of adoption, 53–57, 59–62
    understanding of reproduction, 57–59
prostitution, 105–107, 168–170

Race, Color, and the Young Child, 28
racial and ethnic awareness and identity, 7, 28, 46–50, 66–71,
    148–155, 190–196
racial prejudice and discrimination, 46, 48–50, 145–150, 193–195
Raising Adopted Children, 246
rape, 105–107, 170
reproduction, 56–62
Resolve, Inc., 13, 230, 245
Rillera, Mary Jo, 225
River of Promise, 34
Rocking the Cradle, 34

school personnel, 155–158
Schroen, Susan, 135
search and reunion (see adolescents, desire to meet birthparents;
    birthparents, contact with minor child)
The Search for Anna Fisher, 225
Searching for Minors, 225
sexual abuse (see abuse, child)
siblings, 44–46, 141–145, 179
Social Science Education Consortium, 157
Sorosky, Arthur D., 201, 225
stepparent adoption (see adoption, by stepparent)
Stingley, James, 232
surrogacy (see adoption, through surrogacy)